SHE STOOPS

THE MISTAKES OF A NIGHT

Crofts Classics

GENERAL EDITORS

Samuel H. Beer, *Harvard University*

O. B. Hardison, Jr., *The Folger Shakespeare Library*

OLIVER GOLDSMITH

She Stoops to Conquer

or

The Mistakes of a Night

❧

EDITED BY

Katharine C. Balderston

WELLESLEY COLLEGE

❧

AHM Publishing Corporation
Arlington Heights, Illinois 60004

ISBN: 0-88295-039-8
(Formerly 0-390-22540-0)

Library of Congress Card Number: 51-6755

PRINTED IN THE UNITED STATES OF AMERICA
778
Eleventh Printing

INTRODUCTION

History BEFORE Oliver Goldsmith produced his famous comedy *She Stoops to Conquer*, first played at Covent Garden Theater on March 15, 1773, he had previously written only one other play, *The Good-Natured Man*. Not the least of his triumphs is that, with so little experience in dramatic writing, his second attempt turned out a masterpiece. With *She Stoops to Conquer* he added a play to the perennial repertory of the English-speaking stage. Only a few plays of the eighteenth century—Gay's *Beggar's Opera* and Sheridan's *Rivals* and *The School for Scandal*—share this distinction of continuing popular favor. Goldsmith was not thinking of future fame, however, but of earning money by it (he was, as usual, in debt), and of striking a blow in defense of "laughing comedy" against the popular "sentimental comedy" favored by contemporary audiences. The play's instantaneous success, the fact that the brilliant Sheridan later took up the cudgels in the same cause, and the general love which Goldsmith's critics and biographers bear him, have created a legend that he killed off sentimental comedy by that night's work. But in our own time Ernest Bernbaum has ably demonstrated[1] that this was not the case. The eighteenth-century public was too far gone in its sentimental disease to be so easily cured. If Goldsmith's play is a masterpiece it is so in its own timeless right, and not because it permanently affected the development of English comedy.

The history of the play's production is itself a comedy. After the author had spent months in the country composing it, "strolling about the hedges studying jests with a tragical countenance," neither of the two theatrical managers on whom its fortunes depended would accept it.

[1] Ernest Bernbaum, *The Drama of Sensibility* (Boston, 1915), chaps. xii, xiii

Goldsmith submitted it first to Colman, the manager of Covent Garden, but he kept it so long and raised so many timid objections to it that the offended author took it to Garrick, who controlled Drury Lane. Garrick too proved lukewarm, and at that point Goldsmith's friends stepped in and reopened negotiations with Colman, who, as Dr. Johnson later said, "was prevailed on at last by much solicitation, nay, a kind of force, to bring it on." At rehearsal it underwent other indignities, galling to Goldsmith's pride. The actors designed for the parts of Marlow and Tony Lumpkin, infected by Colman's fears of a fiasco, refused their assignments, and others had to be substituted. The dialogue and plot were under constant fire, and revisions were forced on the humbled author, even after the first night's performance. The two chief actresses quarrelled over who was to speak the epilogue. The epilogue itself caused infinite trouble, and Goldsmith made three tries before he produced one that both Colman and the temperamental Mrs. Bulkley (the Kate Hardcastle of the piece) would accept. The very title was undecided until the day before the opening—the play being advertised under its secondary title, *The Mistakes of a Night*. Meanwhile the newspapers had got wind of the furore behind the scenes and took sides with much throwing about of brains. On the night of the first performance Goldsmith was so nervous lest his play fail and blow up like a barrel of gunpowder, as Colman had predicted, that he is reported to have been found wandering in St. James's Park, and was brought back just in time for the fifth act. The only explosion he heard, however, was the roar of enthusiastic applause. The play was a blazing success. This happy ending was crowned by a command performance for the King and Queen on May 5, and by three profitable author's benefit nights, which brought Goldsmith between four and five hundred pounds. It was published on March 26, with a dedication to Dr. Johnson, who had been its staunchest supporter and most discerning critic throughout.

Significance What was there about this fresh and delightful play that made even two such experienced men of the theater as Colman and Garrick doubtful of its success with the English public? To understand their misgivings, one must know something about the state of public taste and current theatrical fashions, as well as about the underlying ideas that had shaped them.

In the first place, the eighteenth century had developed a passion for gentility, a kind of false decorum which insisted upon elegance of behavior and language in life and in literature. Literature was written for the polite world, and only the strictest propriety and gentility were supposed to please that world. Common human nature, rough jokes, boisterousness, and anything that smacked of the vulgar were frowned upon as "low." Goldsmith hated this stilted ideal, and part of his purpose in writing the play was to bring back into dramatic favor plain speech and natural behavior, in all its robust variety, including the ungenteel. Old Diggory, who guffaws at his master's stories, and the illiterate Tony Lumpkin and his loutish cronies at the Three Pigeons, and even Kate's masquerade as a barmaid, were deliberate affronts to this overrefined squeamishness of the age. Goldsmith makes his point ironically, but unmistakably, in the remark of Tony's boon companion who loves to hear him sing "bekeays he never gives us nothing that's *low*." It was, in fact, the hearty "lowness" of much of the play that aroused Colman's worst fears.

The second, and historically more important, protest the play embodies is against the concept of sentimentalism, which has already been referred to. Sentimentalism is not identical with gentility, though sometimes confused with it because they flourished together. It is basically a view of life, rather than a mode of social behavior, and consists in a faith that man, foolish and erring as he is, is yet basically goodhearted, and that the way to reclaim him is to appeal, not to his head, but to his heart. This concept differed radically from the Christian and classic view of man, which insisted on the duality of his nature, compounded of animal evil and spiritual good, "created part to fall and part to rise," and on the supreme rôle of reason as the only reliable guide of the free will to virtuous action. This older view underlay the classic theory of comedy which Ben Jonson had handed on to the Restoration playwrights. To them, the purpose of comedy was to expose, by hardheaded, satirical ridicule, the follies and vices of men, so that the audience, in laughing at the weaknesses of others, would learn to know their own. In this view, ridicule was curative, and ridicule was the business of comedy. But in the year 1696, an audience which had gone to see a new comedy by Colley Cibber, *Love's Last Shift*, were amazed to find themselves happily weeping, instead of laughing, when in the fifth act the erring husband and wife repented their behavior and were touchingly reconciled. This was the first sentimental comedy. The deeper ethical implications of this new way of making comedy "teach delightfully" were doubtless not apparent either to Cibber or to his audience; the play was merely a random experiment. But it contained the germ of an idea which was later to flourish mightily, both in literature and in serious thought. Many historical factors combined at the start of the eighteenth century to encourage a new optimism and complacency about human nature, the most outstanding being the philosophical writings of Lord Shaftesbury, who, in his *Inquiry Concerning Virtue or Merit* (1709), and later works, eloquently demonstrated not only that man was innately good, but that in being so he upheld the harmonious plan of a perfect universe. After Shaftesbury, the sentimental view invaded all forms of literature, and life itself. The history of its progress, checked but not defeated by such doughty opponents as Swift, Bishop Butler, Burke, and Dr. Johnson, may fairly be called the central ideological conflict of the eighteenth century. Literary historians have assigned to it a major rôle in the transition from the classic to the romantic temper. Social historians have credited it with inspiring the great humanitarian reforms of the age.

But if the long-range results of the changed attitude toward man's fundamental nature were on the whole beneficent, its immediate impact on drama was not. The playwrights who exploited it tried to present delicate and exalted feeling without exploring deeply the real psychology of the emotions. In the world they created of innocent sufferers and profligates melted into virtue by noble example, the tender heart became the sole criterion of virtue. As Goldsmith himself said of these sentimental characters, "if they happen to have faults or foibles, the spectator is taught, not only to pardon, but to applaud them, in consideration of the goodness of their hearts; so that folly, instead of being ridiculed, is commended." It was a type of drama which lacked the moral realism and ethical value of both tragedy and true comedy, but which borrowed from both. The audience could indulge in the luxury of tears, and yet keep the happy ending, and go away comfortably flattered about the amiability of their species.

But though Goldsmith saw clearly enough the fatuousness of this sentimental morality, he does not actually meet the problem squarely in *She Stoops to Conquer*. He is content to restore to comedy her birthright of laughter without attempting to teach any overt lesson. Nobody is reformed here, either by sentimental tears or by satirical ridicule, for, in the last analysis, nobody (with the possible exception of the egregious Mrs. Hardcastle) seriously needs reforming. They are all amiable or lovably ridiculous, and our laughter is not scornful but sympathetic. To find its parallel we must go back, not to the comedy of the Restoration, which Goldsmith professed to imitate, but to Shakespeare himself. Goldsmith, like Shakespeare, could find human nature absurd and yet recognize his own kinship to it. His very temperament, compounded of a tender heart and a clear insight, kept him from both extremes of sentimentalism and satire, and produced instead, as that combination alone may, the true humor which sees all and forgives all. But, although Goldsmith refuses to go the whole way by adopting the satirist's attitude in his protest against sentimentalism, he does keep up a skirmishing fight with it along the sidelines. Marlow cuts a ridiculous figure at Kate's hands when he tries a "sober, sentimental interview" with her; and when later, in Act IV, he makes his "noble" renunciation of her in her character as barmaid, she describes it later as a "tragedy speech" and "pretended rapture." When Hastings and Miss Neville throw themselves, in the best sentimental tradition, on the mercy and humanity of her guardians, Mrs. Hardcastle cuts them off with a comparison to "the whining end of a modern novel." Sentimental flights are inserted only to be punctured by the weapon of comic realism.

The play has often been described as farcical, because the central situation—Marlow's mistaking Mr. Hardcastle's house for an inn—rests on a mere mistake, and an improbable one at that. There is justice in this charge. The dialogue has to be very consciously manipulated in order to sustain the misunderstanding plausibly until the fourth act; but the skill with which Goldsmith does it is one of the play's minor triumphs. In the last analysis, however, the action springs more from character than from mere situation, and the play may more justly be described as high comedy with farcical complications. Mr. Hardcastle with his oldfashioned politeness, his silly wife, the saucy, quick-witted Kate, bashful Mr. Marlow, and the immortal bumpkin Tony are all rounded, living, consistent people; and their characters determine the plot, even to the original farcical mistake, for that would never have occurred but for Tony's love of a practical joke. Tony is the play's most original character, and might be called the uncrowned hero of it; for, beside giving Kate her opportunity to win her man, he solves the other lovers' problem as well by his mother-wit. When he finally discovers his own age, his triumphant escape from his mother's apronstrings ends the play on just the right note of joyous, comic absurdity.

Sources Until recently, Goldsmith's editors have been content with the story, first told by his sister Mrs. Hodson,[2] of Goldsmith's having founded the central situation of the play—Marlow's mistaking Mr. Hardcastle's house for an inn—on a similar blunder of his own youth in the house of one Mr. Featherstone of Ardagh. It was retold by all his biographers, who saw in it a delightful example of Goldsmith's well-known habit of attributing his own experiences to his brain-children. Mrs. Hodson's circumstantial account can hardly be discredited, especially since Prior, in his *Life of Goldsmith*,[3] recounts an independent, if somewhat hazy, confirmation of it from the grandson of the Mr. Featherstone in question. However, Mr. Mark Schorer[4] has recently pointed out a striking resemblance between Marlow's "mistake," including the whole scene in which he orders his dinner, to an episode in Susanna Centlivre's comedy, *The Man's Bewitch'd; or The Devil to Do About Her* (1709). There is no basic contradiction in-

[2] See *The Collected Letters of Oliver Goldsmith*, ed. K. C. Balderston (Cambridge, 1928), Appendix III, pp. 166-68
[3] *The Life of Oliver Goldsmith, M.B.* (London, 1837), Vol. I. pp. 45-7   [4] See Bibliography, p. 73

volved, however, in accepting both possibilities. Another possible literary source has been suggested by Mr. A. L. Sells,[5] in the resemblance of Kate's stratagem of masquerading as a servant, in order to discover the character of her lover, to a parallel situation in Marivaux's *Le Jeu de l'Amour et du Hasarde* (1730); and Mr. Maurice Baudin[5] has persuasively argued for an even closer resemblance to the same stratagem employed by the heroine of Le Grand's *Galant Coureur* (1722). But though Goldsmith may have utilized these hints from older plays, it is well to bear in mind that the merit of inventing the episodes of a plot is a minor one. Shakespeare borrowed all his plots. Goldsmith reshaped his borrowed materials into a play which lives through the touch of his genius, while the plays he borrowed from gather dust upon the shelves.

[5] See Bibliography, p. 73

PRINCIPAL DATES IN THE LIFE OF OLIVER GOLDSMITH [6]

1730   (Nov. 10, Old Style) Born at Pallas, County Longford, Ireland, one of seven children of the Rev. Charles Goldsmith and Ann Jones. Schooling at Elphin, Athlone, and Edgesworthstown.

1745   (June 11) Enters Trinity College, Dublin, as a sizer, or scholarship student.

1750   (Feb. 27) Receives his A.B. from Trinity College.

1750-52   Lives with his relatives, wavers between the church and the law as his profession, finally settles on medicine.

1752   (Oct.) Enters the medical school of Edinburgh University.

1754   (Feb. 10) Goes to Leyden, to continue his medical studies.

1755-6   Wanders over Europe on foot.

1756   Returns, and settles in London.

1756-9   Practices medicine, teaches school at Peckham, reviews books for *The Monthly Review,* considers going to India as a physician.

1759   Publishes his first book, *An Enquiry into the Present State of Polite Learning in Europe.* Begins his acquaintance with literary circles.

1760-61   Meets Johnson, contributes *Chinese Letters* to Newberry's *Public Ledger* (published in 1762 under the title *A Citizen of the World*).

[6] This outline does not include Goldsmith's large output of literary hack-work—histories, abridgments, translations, etc.—by which he eked out his income

1764   Publishes his long poem, *The Traveller*. Is elected a charter member of Dr. Johnson's Club, "to represent literature."

1765   Collects and publishes his *Essays*.

1766   Publishes his novel, *The Vicar of Wakefield*.

1768   Produces his first play, *The Good-Natured Man*, at Covent Garden.

1770   Publishes *The Deserted Village*. Visits Paris with the Hornecks.

1773   Produces *She Stoops to Conquer* at Covent Garden.

1774   Writes *Retaliation*, left unfinished at his death. Dies on April 4, in his chambers in the Temple.

SHE STOOPS TO CONQUER

or

The Mistakes of a Night

❧

DEDICATION

TO SAMUEL JOHNSON, LL.D.

DEAR SIR,

By inscribing this slight performance to you, I do not mean so much to compliment you as myself. It may do me some honor to inform the public, that I have lived many years in intimacy with you.[1] It may serve the interests of mankind also to inform them, that the greatest wit may be found in a character, without impairing the most unaffected piety.

I have, particularly, reason to thank you for your partiality to this performance. The undertaking a comedy, not merely sentimental, was very dangerous; and Mr. Colman, who saw this piece in its various stages, always thought it so. However, I ventured to trust it to the public; and though it was necessarily delayed till late in the season, I have every reason to be grateful.

I am, dear sir,
Your most sincere friend,
And admirer,
OLIVER GOLDSMITH

[1] They had known each other at least since 1761, and Goldsmith was an original member of Johnson's famous Club, founded in 1764

PROLOGUE

BY DAVID GARRICK, ESQ.[2]

(*Enter* MR. WOODWARD,[3] *dressed in black, and holding
a handkerchief to his eyes*)

Excuse me, sirs, I pray—I can't yet speak—
I'm crying now—and have been all the week!
" 'Tis not alone this mourning suit," good masters;
"I've that within" [4]—for which there are no plasters!
Pray would you know the reason why I'm crying?
The Comic Muse, long sick, is now a-dying!
And if she goes, my tears will never stop;
For, as a player, I can't squeeze out one drop;
I am undone, that's all—shall lose my bread—
I'd rather, but that's nothing—lose my head.
When the sweet maid is laid upon the bier,
Shuter and I shall be chief mourners here.
To her a mawkish drab of spurious breed,
Who deals in *sentimentals*, will succeed!
Poor Ned [5] and I are dead to all intents;
We can as soon speak Greek as *sentiments!*
Both nervous grown, to keep our spirits up,
We now and then take down a hearty cup.
What shall we do?—If Comedy forsake us!
They'll turn us out, and no one else will take us.
But why can't I be moral?—Let me try:
My heart thus pressing—fix'd my face and eye—
With a sententious look, that nothing means
(Faces are blocks in sentimental scenes),
Thus I begin—"All is not gold that glitters,
Pleasure seems sweet, but proves a glass of bitters.
When ignorance enters, folly is at hand;

[2] Garrick contributed this prologue to make amends for his
previous coolness toward the play. See the Introduction, p. vi
[3] The comedian who had refused to play the part of Tony
Lumpkin. See the Introduction, p. vi   [4] 'Tis not alone . . .
that within adapted from *Hamlet*, I, ii, 77-85   [5] Ned Edward
Shuter, the actor who played Hardcastle

Learning is better far than house and land.
Let not your virtue trip; who trips may stumble,
And virtue is not virtue, if she tumble."
   I give it up—morals won't do for me;
To make you laugh, I must play tragedy.
One hope remains,—hearing the maid was ill,
A *doctor*[6] comes this night to show his skill.
To cheer her heart, and give your muscles motion,
He, in *five draughts* prepared, presents a potion:
A kind of magic charm—for be assured,
If you will swallow it, the maid is cured:
But desperate the Doctor, and her case is,
If you reject the dose, and make wry faces!
This truth he boasts, will boast it while he lives,
No poisonous drugs are mixed in what he gives.
Should he succeed, you'll give him his degree;
If not, within he will receive no fee!
The college *you*, must his pretensions back,
Pronounce him *regular*, or dub him *quack*.

---

[6] Doctor Goldsmith's claim to this title has been disputed as no record exists of his having taken the degree of M.D.; he used it consistently however after 1763

DRAMATIS PERSONAE

SIR CHARLES MARLOW
YOUNG MARLOW (his son)
HARDCASTLE
HASTINGS
TONY LUMPKIN
DIGGORY

MRS. HARDCASTLE
MISS HARDCASTLE
MISS NEVILLE
MAID

LANDLORD, SERVANTS, &c.

SHE STOOPS TO CONQUER

or

The Mistakes of a Night

Act I

❧

SCENE I. *A Chamber in an Old-Fashioned House*

(*Enter* MRS. HARDCASTLE *and* MR. HARDCASTLE)

MRS. HARDCASTLE. I vow, Mr. Hardcastle, you're very particular. Is there a creature in the whole country, but ourselves, that does not take a trip to town now and then, to rub off the rust a little? There's the two Miss Hoggs, and our neighbor, Mrs. Grigsby, go to take a month's polishing every winter.

HARDCASTLE. Ay, and bring back vanity and affectation to last them the whole year. I wonder why London cannot keep its own fools at home. In my time, the follies of the town crept slowly among us, but now they travel faster than a stagecoach. Its fopperies come down, not only as inside passengers, but in the very basket.[1]

MRS. HARDCASTLE. Ay, *your* times were fine times, indeed; you have been telling us of *them* for many a long year. Here we live in an old rumbling mansion, that looks for all the world like an inn, but that we never see company. Our best visitors are old Mrs. Oddfish, the curate s wife, and little Cripplegate, the lame dancing master; and all our entertainment your old stories of Prince Eugene and the Duke of Marlborough.[2] I hate such old-fashioned trumpery.

[1] basket a compartment overhanging the rear axle, for carrying luggage and excess passengers [2] Prince Eugene . . . Marlborough Prince Eugene of Savoie and John Churchill, Duke of Marlborough, were the generals who led the Allied armies against Louis XIV and defeated him in the War of the Spanish Succession (1701-13); Hardcastle's many references to them show him living in the glories of the past

1

HARDCASTLE. And I love it. I love everything that's old: old friends, old times, old manners, old books, old wine; and, I believe, Dorothy, (*taking her hand*) you'll own I have been pretty fond of an old wife.

MRS. HARDCASTLE. Lord, Mr. Hardcastle, you're forever at your Dorothys and your old wifes. You may be a Darby, but I'll be no Joan, I promise you. I'm not so old as you'd make me by more than one good year. Add twenty to twenty, and make money of that.

HARDCASTLE. Let me see; twenty added to twenty, makes just fifty and seven.

MRS. HARDCASTLE. It's false, Mr. Hardcastle; I was but twenty when I was brought to bed of Tony, that I had by Mr. Lumpkin, my first husband; and he's not come to years of discretion yet.

HARDCASTLE. Nor ever will, I dare answer for him. Ay, you have taught *him* finely!

MRS. HARDCASTLE. No matter, Tony Lumpkin has a good fortune. My son is not to live by his learning. I don't think a boy wants much learning to spend fifteen hundred a year.

HARDCASTLE. Learning, quotha! [3] a mere composition of tricks and mischief!

MRS. HARDCASTLE. Humor, my dear; nothing but humor. Come, Mr. Hardcastle, you must allow the boy a little humor.

HARDCASTLE. I'd sooner allow him a horsepond. If burning the footmen's shoes, frighting the maids, and worrying the kittens, be humor, he has it. It was but yesterday he fastened my wig to the back of my chair, and when I went to make a bow, I popped my bald head in Mrs. Frizzle's face.

MRS. HARDCASTLE. And I am to blame? The poor boy was always too sickly to do any good. A school would be his death. When he comes to be a little stronger, who knows what a year or two's Latin may do for him?

HARDCASTLE. Latin for him! A cat and fiddle! No, no, the alehouse and the stable are the only schools he'll ever go to.

MRS. HARDCASTLE. Well, we must not snub the poor boy now, for I believe we shan't have him long among us.

[3] **quotha!** nonsense!

Anybody that looks in his face may see he's consumptive.

HARDCASTLE. Ay, if growing too fat be one of the symptoms.

MRS. HARDCASTLE. He coughs sometimes.

HARDCASTLE. Yes, when his liquor goes the wrong way.

MRS. HARDCASTLE. I'm actually afraid of his lungs.

HARDCASTLE. And truly, so am I; for he sometimes whoops like a speaking trumpet—(TONY *hallooing behind the scenes*) O there he goes—a very consumptive figure, truly.

(Enter TONY, crossing the stage)

MRS. HARDCASTLE. Tony, where are you going, my charmer? Won't you give papa and I a little of your company, lovey?

TONY. I'm in haste, mother; I cannot stay.

MRS. HARDCASTLE. You shan't venture out this raw evening, my dear; you look most shockingly.

TONY. I can't stay, I tell you. The Three Pigeons expects me down every moment. There's some fun going forward.

HARDCASTLE. Ay, the alehouse, the old place; I thought so.

MRS. HARDCASTLE. A low, paltry set of fellows.

TONY. Not so low neither. There's Dick Muggins the exciseman,[4] Jack Slang the horse doctor, little Aminadab that grinds the music box, and Tom Twist that spins the pewter platter.

MRS. HARDCASTLE. Pray, my dear, disappoint them for one night at least.

TONY. As for disappointing *them,* I should not so much mind; but I can't abide to disappoint *myself.*

MRS. HARDCASTLE. *(Detaining him)* You shan't go.

TONY. I will, I tell you.

MRS. HARDCASTLE. I say you shan't.

TONY. We'll see which is the strongest, you or I.

(Exit, hauling her out)

HARDCASTLE. *(Alone)* Ay, there goes a pair that only spoil each other. But is not the whole age in a combination to drive sense and discretion out of doors? There's my pretty darling Kate; the fashions of the times have almost infected her too. By living a year or two in town, she is

⁴ **exciseman** taxcollector

as fond of gauze, and French frippery, as the best of them.

(*Enter* MISS HARDCASTLE)

Blessings on my pretty innocence! Dressed out as usual, my Kate. Goodness! what a quantity of superfluous silk hast thou got about thee, girl! I could never teach the fools of this age that the indigent world could be clothed out of the trimmings of the vain.

MISS HARDCASTLE. You know our agreement, sir. You allow me the morning to receive and pay visits, and to dress in my own manner; and in the evening, I put on my housewife's dress to please you.

HARDCASTLE. Well, remember I insist on the terms of our agreement; and, by the bye, I believe I shall have occasion to try your obedience this very evening.

MISS HARDCASTLE. I protest, sir, I don't comprehend your meaning.

HARDCASTLE. Then, to be plain with you, Kate, I expect the young gentleman I have chosen to be your husband from town this very day. I have his father's letter, in which he informs me his son is set out, and that he intends to follow himself shortly after.

MISS HARDCASTLE. Indeed! I wish I had known something of this before. Bless me, how shall I behave? It's a thousand to one I shan't like him; our meeting will be so formal, and so like a thing of business, that I shall find no room for friendship or esteem.

HARDCASTLE. Depend upon it, child, I'll never control your choice; but Mr. Marlow, whom I have pitched upon, is the son of my old friend, Sir Charles Marlow, of whom you have heard me talk so often. The young gentleman has been bred a scholar, and is designed for an employment in the service of his country. I am told he's a man of an excellent understanding.

MISS HARDCASTLE. Is he?

HARDCASTLE. Very generous.

MISS HARDCASTLE. I believe I shall like him.

HARDCASTLE. Young and brave.

MISS HARDCASTLE. I'm sure I shall like him.

HARDCASTLE. And very handsome.

MISS HARDCASTLE. My dear papa, say no more (*kissing his hand*), he's mine, I'll have him.

HARDCASTLE. And to crown all, Kate, he's one of the most bashful and reserved young fellows in all the world.

MISS HARDCASTLE. Eh! you have frozen me to death again. That word reserved has undone all the rest of his accomplishments. A reserved lover, it is said, always makes a suspicious husband.

HARDCASTLE. On the contrary, modesty seldom resides in a breast that is not enriched with nobler virtues. It was the very feature in his character that first struck me.

MISS HARDCASTLE. He must have more striking features to catch me, I promise you. However, if he be so young, so handsome, and so everything as you mention, I believe he'll do still. I think I'll have him.

HARDCASTLE. Ay, Kate, but there is still an obstacle. It's more than an even wager, he may not have *you*.

MISS HARDCASTLE. My dear papa, why will you mortify one so? Well, if he refuses, instead of breaking my heart at his indifference, I'll only break my glass for its flattery, set my cap to some newer fashion, and look out for some less difficult admirer.

HARDCASTLE. Bravely resolved! In the meantime I'll go prepare the servants for his reception; as we seldom see company, they want as much training as a company of recruits the first day's muster.   (*Exit*)

MISS HARDCASTLE. (*Alone*) Lud,[5] this news of papa's puts me all in a flutter. Young, handsome; these he put last, but I put them foremost. Sensible, good-natured; I like all that. But then, reserved and sheepish; that's much against him. Yet can't he be cured of his timidity by being taught to be proud of his wife? Yes, and can't I—but I vow I'm disposing of the husband, before I have secured the lover.

(*Enter* MISS NEVILLE.)

MISS HARDCASTLE. I'm glad you're come, Neville, my dear. Tell me, Constance, how do I look this evening? Is there anything whimsical about me? Is it one of my well-looking days, child? Am I in face to-day?

MISS NEVILLE. Perfectly, my dear. Yet, now I look again

[5] Lud Lord, a customary euphemism of the period to avoid breaking the first commandment, like "egad" and "ecod" (by God) and "zounds" (by God's wounds) found throughout the play

—bless me!—sure, no accident has happened among the canary birds or the goldfishes? Has your brother or the cat been meddling? Or has the last novel been too moving?

MISS HARDCASTLE. No; nothing of all this. I have been threatened—I can scarce get it out—I have been threatened with a lover.

MISS NEVILLE. And his name—

MISS HARDCASTLE. Is Marlow.

MISS NEVILLE. Indeed!

MISS HARDCASTLE. The son of Sir Charles Marlow.

MISS NEVILLE. As I live, the most intimate friend of Mr. Hastings, *my* admirer. They are never asunder. I believe you must have seen him when we lived in town.

MISS HARDCASTLE. Never.

MISS NEVILLE. He's a very singular character, I assure you. Among women of reputation and virtue, he is the modestest man alive; but his acquaintance give him a very different character among creatures of another stamp: you understand me.

MISS HARDCASTLE. An odd character, indeed. I shall never be able to manage him. What shall I do? Pshaw, think no more of him, but trust to occurrences for success. But how goes on your own affair, my dear? Has my mother been courting you for my brother Tony, as usual?

MISS NEVILLE. I have just come from one of our agreeable *tête-à-têtes*. She has been saying a hundred tender things, and setting off her pretty monster as the very pink of perfection.

MISS HARDCASTLE. And her partiality is such, that she actually thinks him so. A fortune like yours is no small temptation. Besides, as she has the sole management of it, I'm not surprised to see her unwilling to let it go out of the family.

MISS NEVILLE. A fortune like mine, which chiefly consists in jewels, is no such mighty temptation. But at any rate if my dear Hastings be but constant, I make no doubt to be too hard for her at last. However, I let her suppose that I am in love with her son, and she never once dreams that my affections are fixed upon another.

MISS HARDCASTLE. My good brother holds out stoutly. I could almost love him for hating you so.

MISS NEVILLE. It is a good-natured creature at bottom,

and I'm sure would wish to see me married to anybody but himself. But my aunt's bell rings for our afternoon's walk round the improvements. *Allons.*[6] Courage is necessary, as our affairs are critical.

MISS HARDCASTLE. Would it were bedtime and all were well.[7]   (*Exeunt*)

SCENE II. *An Alehouse Room*

(*Several shabby fellows with punch and tobacco.* TONY *at the head of the table, a little higher than the rest; a mallet in his hand*)

OMNES. Hurrea, hurrea, hurrea, bravo!

FIRST FELLOW. Now gentlemen, silence for a song. The Squire is going to knock himself down[1] for a song.

OMNES. Ay, a song, a song!

TONY. Then I'll sing you, gentlemen, a song I made upon this alehouse, The Three Pigeons.

SONG

Let schoolmasters puzzle their brain,
  With grammar, and nonsense, and learning;
Good liquor, I stoutly maintain,
  Gives genus[2] a better discerning.
Let them brag of their heathenish gods,
  Their Lethes, their Styxes, and Stygians,
Their quis, and their quæs, and their quods,[3]
  They're all but a parcel of pigeons.[4]
                 Toroddle, toroddle, toroll.

When Methodist[5] preachers come down,
  A-preaching that drinking is sinful,
I'll wager the rascals a crown,
  They always preach best with a skinful.
But when you come down with your pence,
  For a slice of their scurvy religion,
I'll leave it to all men of sense,
  But you my good friend are the pigeon.
                 Toroddle, toroddle, toroll.

[6] Allons Forward   [7] Would . . . all well Falstaff's remark in *I Henry IV*, V, i, 126   [1] knock himself down nominate himself   [2] genus Tony's version of "genius"   [3] Lethes . . . quods he makes a hash of all the classical words he knows   [4] pigeons dupes   [5] Methodist Methodism, founded by John Wesley in 1739, was looked down on by the orthodox upper classes

Then come, put the jorum[*] about,
    And let us be merry and clever,
Our hearts and our liquors are stout,
    Here's the Three Jolly Pigeons forever.
Let some cry up woodcock or hare,
    Your bustards, your ducks, and your widgeons;
But of all the birds in the air,
    Here's a health to the Three Jolly Pigeons.
                  Toroddle, toroddle, toroll.

OMNES. Bravo, bravo!

FIRST FELLOW. The Squire has got spunk in him.

SECOND FELLOW. I loves to hear him sing, bekeays he never gives us nothing that's *low*.

THIRD FELLOW. O damn anything that's *low*, I cannot bear it.

FOURTH FELLOW. The genteel thing is the genteel thing at any time; if so be that a gentleman bees in a concatenation accordingly.

THIRD FELLOW. I like the maxum of it, Master Muggins. What though I am obligated to dance a bear, a man may be a gentleman for all that. May this be my poison if my bear ever dances but to the very genteelest of tunes:[7] Water Parted,[8] or the Minuet in Ariadne.[9]

SECOND FELLOW. What a pity it is the Squire is not come to his own. It would be well for all the publicans within ten miles round of him.

TONY. Ecod and so it would Master Slang. I'd then show what it was to keep choice of company.

SECOND FELLOW. O he takes after his own father for that. To be sure, old Squire Lumpkin was the finest gentleman I ever set my eyes on. For winding the straight horn, or beating a thicket for a hare, or a wench, he never had his fellow. It was a saying in the place, that he kept the best horses, dogs, and girls in the whole county.

TONY. Ecod, and when I'm of age I'll be no bastard, I promise you. I have been thinking of Bet Bouncer and the miller's gray mare to begin with. But come, my boys, drink

---

[*] jorum punchbowl [7] I loves . . . genteelest of tunes for the ridicule of gentility here see the Introduction, p. vii [8] Water Parted an air in Arne's opera *Artaxerxes* [9] Minuet in Ariadne the opening music in Handel's opera *Ariadne*

about and be merry, for you pay no reckoning. Well, Stingo, what's the matter?

(*Enter* LANDLORD)

LANDLORD. There be two gentlemen in a post chaise[10] at the door. They have lost their way upo' the forest; and they are talking something about Mr. Hardcastle.

TONY. As sure as can be, one of them must be the gentleman that's coming down to court my sister. Do they seem to be Londoners?

LANDLORD. I believe they may. They look woundily[11] like Frenchmen.

TONY. Then desire them to step this way, and I'll set them right in a twinkling.   (*Exit* LANDLORD)
Gentlemen, as they may n't be good enough company for you, step down for a moment, and I'll be with you in the squeezing of a lemon.   (*Exeunt mob*)

TONY. (*Alone*) Father-in-law has been calling me whelp, and hound, this half year. Now, if I pleased, I could be so revenged upon the old grumbletonian. But then I'm afraid, —afraid of what? I shall soon be worth fifteen hundred a year, and let him frighten me out of *that* if he can.

(*Enter* LANDLORD, *conducting* MARLOW *and* HASTINGS)

MARLOW. What a tedious, uncomfortable day have we had of it! We were told it was but forty miles across the country, and we have come above threescore.

HASTINGS. And all, Marlow, from that unaccountable reserve of yours, that would not let us enquire more frequently on the way.

MARLOW. I own, Hastings, I am unwilling to lay myself under an obligation to everyone I meet, and often stand the chance of an unmannerly answer.

HASTINGS. At present, however, we are not likely to receive any answer.

TONY. No offense, gentlemen. But I'm told you have been enquiring for one Mr. Hardcastle, in these parts. Do you know what part of the country you are in?

HASTINGS. Not in the least, sir, but should thank you for information.

[10] **post chaise** a hired carriage drawn by relays of horses for rapid travel   [11] **woundily** extremely

TONY. Nor the way you came?

HASTINGS. No, sir; but if you can inform us—

TONY. Why, gentlemen, if you know neither the road you are going, nor where you are, nor the road you came, the first thing I have to inform you is, that—you have lost your way.

MARLOW. We wanted no ghost[12] to tell us that.

TONY. Pray, gentlemen, may I be so bold as to ask the place from whence you came?

MARLOW. That's not necessary towards directing us where we are to go.

TONY. No offense; but question for question is all fair, you know. Pray, gentlemen, is not this same Hardcastle a cross-grained, old-fashioned, whimsical fellow, with an ugly face, a daughter, and a pretty son?

HASTINGS. We have not seen the gentleman, but he has the family you mention.

TONY. The daughter, a tall, trapesing, trolloping,[13] talkative maypole; the son, a pretty, well-bred, agreeable youth, that everybody is fond of.

MARLOW. Our information differs in this. The daughter is said to be well-bred and beautiful; the son an awkward booby, reared up and spoiled at his mother's apron string.

TONY. He-he-hem!—Then, gentlemen, all I have to tell you is, that you won't reach Mr. Hardcastle's house this night, I believe.

HASTINGS. Unfortunate!

TONY. It's a damned long, dark, boggy, dirty, dangerous way. Stingo, tell the gentlemen the way to Mr. Hardcastle's; (*winking upon the* LANDLORD) Mr. Hardcastle's of Quagmire Marsh, you understand me.

LANDLORD. Master Hardcastle's! Lack-a-daisy, my masters, you're come a deadly deal wrong! When you came to the bottom of the hill, you should have crossed down Squash Lane.

MARLOW. Cross down Squash Lane!

LANDLORD. Then you were to keep straight forward, till you came to four roads.

MARLOW. Come to where four roads meet!

[12] **We wanted no ghost** see *Hamlet*, I, v, 125   [13] **trolloping** slovenly

TONY. Ay; but you must be sure to take only one of them.

MARLOW. O sir, you're facetious.

TONY. Then keeping to the right, you are to go sideways till you come upon Crack-skull Common: there you must look sharp for the track of the wheel, and go forward, till you come to farmer Murrain's barn. Coming to the farmer's barn, you are to turn to the right, and then to the left, and then to the right about again, till you find out the old mill—

MARLOW. Zounds, man! we could as soon find out the longitude! [14]

HASTINGS. What's to be done, Marlow?

MARLOW. This house promises but a poor reception; though perhaps the landlord can accommodate us.

LANDLORD. Alack, master, we have but one spare bed in the whole house.

TONY. And to my knowledge, that's taken up by three lodgers already. (*After a pause in which the rest seem disconcerted*) I have hit it. Don't you think, Stingo, our landlady could accommodate the gentlemen by the fireside, with—three chairs and a bolster?

HASTINGS. I hate sleeping by the fireside.

MARLOW. And I detest your three chairs and a bolster.

TONY. You do, do you?—then, let me see—what—if you go on a mile further, to the Buck's Head; the old Buck's Head on the hill, one of the best inns in the whole county?

HASTINGS. O ho! so we have escaped an adventure for this night, however.

LANDLORD. (*Apart to* TONY) Sure, you ben't sending them to your father's as an inn, be you?

TONY. Mum, you fool you. Let *them* find that out. (*To them*) You have only to keep on straight forward, till you come to a large old house by the roadside. You'll see a pair of large horns over the door. That's the sign. Drive up the yard, and call stoutly about you.

HASTINGS. Sir, we are obliged to you. The servants can't miss the way?

[14] **find out the longitude** in 1761 John Harrison had invented an instrument for determining the longitude at sea and claimed the reward of £20,000 offered by Parliament in 1713, which was tardily granted in 1773

TONY. No, no; but I tell you, though, the landlord is rich, and going to leave off business; so he wants to be thought a gentleman, saving your presence, he! he! he! He'll be for giving you his company, and, ecod, if you mind him, he'll persuade you that his mother was an alderman and his aunt a justice of peace.

LANDLORD. A troublesome old blade, to be sure; but a keeps as good wines and beds as any in the whole country.

MARLOW. Well, if he supplies us with these, we shall want no further connection. We are to turn to the right, did you say?

TONY. No, no; straight forward. I'll just step myself, and show you a piece of the way. (*To the* LANDLORD) Mum!

LANDLORD. Ah, bless your heart, for a sweet, pleasant— damn'd mischievous son of a whore. (*Exeunt*)

Act II

SCENE. *An Old-Fashioned House*

(*Enter* HARDCASTLE, *followed by three or four awkward* SERVANTS)

HARDCASTLE. Well, I hope you're perfect in the table exercise I have been teaching you these three days. You all know your posts and your places, and can show that you have been used to good company, without ever stirring from home.

OMNES. Ay, ay.

HARDCASTLE. When company comes, you are not to pop out and stare, and then run in again, like frighted rabbits in a warren.

OMNES. No, no.

HARDCASTLE. You, Diggory, whom I have taken from the barn, are to make a show at the side table; and you, Roger, whom I have advanced from the plow, are to place yourself behind *my* chair. But you're not to stand so, with your hands in your pockets. Take your hands from your pockets, Roger; and from your head, you blockhead, you. See how Diggory carries his hands. They're a little too stiff, indeed, but that's no great matter.

DIGGORY. Ay, mind how I hold them. I learned to hold my hands this way, when I was upon drill for the militia. And so being upon drill—

HARDCASTLE. You must not be so talkative, Diggory. You must be all attention to the guests. You must hear us talk, and not think of talking; you must see us drink, and not think of drinking; you must see us eat, and not think of eating.

DIGGORY. By the laws, your worship, that's parfectly unpossible. Whenever Diggory sees yeating going forward, ecod, he's always wishing for a mouthful himself.

HARDCASTLE. Blockhead! Is not a bellyful in the kitchen as good as a bellyful in the parlor? Stay your stomach with that reflection.

DIGGORY. Ecod, I thank your worship, I'll make a shift to stay my stomach with a slice of cold beef in the pantry.

HARDCASTLE. Diggory, you are too talkative. Then if I happen to say a good thing, or tell a good story at table, you must not all burst out a-laughing, as if you made part of the company.

DIGGORY. Then, ecod, your worship must not tell the story of the Ould Grouse in the gun room; I can't help laughing at that—he! he! he!—for the soul of me. We have laughed at that these twenty years—ha! ha! ha!

HARDCASTLE. Ha! ha! ha! The story is a good one. Well, honest Diggory, you may laugh at that—but still remember to be attentive. Suppose one of the company should call for a glass of wine, how will you behave? A glass of wine, sir, if you please (*To* DIGGORY) Eh, why don't you move?

DIGGORY. Ecod, your worship, I never have courage till I see the eatables and drinkables brought upo' the table, and then I'm as bauld as a lion.

HARDCASTLE. What, will nobody move?

FIRST SERVANT. I'm not to leave this pleace.

SECOND SERVANT. I'm sure it's no pleace of mine.

THIRD SERVANT. Nor mine, for sartain.

DIGGORY. Wauns,[1] and I'm sure it canna be mine.

[1] Wauns Diggory's version of "zounds"; see note on p. 5

HARDCASTLE. You numskulls! and so while, like your betters, you are quarreling for places, the guests must be starved. O you dunces! I find I must begin all over again— But don't I hear a coach drive into the yard? To your posts, you blockheads. I'll go in the meantime, and give my old friend's son a hearty reception at the gate.

(*Exit* HARDCASTLE)

DIGGORY. By the elevens, my pleace is gone quite out my head.

ROGER. I know that my pleace is to be everywhere.

FIRST SERVANT. Where the devil is mine?

SECOND SERVANT. My pleace is to be nowhere at all; and so I'ze go about my business.

(*Exeunt* SERVANTS, *running about as if frighted, different ways*)

(*Enter* SERVANT *with candles, showing in* MARLOW *and* HASTINGS)

SERVANT. Welcome, gentlemen, very welcome! This way.

HASTINGS. After the disappointments of the day, welcome once more, Charles, to the comforts of a clean room and a good fire. Upon my word, a very well-looking house; antique but creditable.

MARLOW. The usual fate of a large mansion. Having first ruined the master by good housekeeping, it at last comes to levy contributions as an inn.

HASTINGS. As you say, we passengers are to be taxed to pay all these fineries. I have often seen a good sideboard, or a marble chimney piece, though not actually put in the bill, inflame a reckoning confoundedly.

MARLOW. Travelers, George, must pay in all places. The only difference is, that in good inns you pay dearly for luxuries; in bad inns, you are fleeced and starved.

HASTINGS. You have lived pretty much among them. In truth, I have been often surprised, that you who have seen so much of the world, with your natural good sense, and your many opportunities, could never yet acquire a requisite share of assurance.

MARLOW. The Englishman's malady. But tell me, George, where could I have learned that assurance you talk of? My life has been chiefly spent in a college or an inn, in seclusion from that lovely part of the creation that chiefly teach men confidence. I don't know that I was ever familiarly acquainted with a single modest woman— except my mother.—But among females of another class, you know—

HASTINGS. Ay, among them you are impudent enough, of all conscience.

MARLOW. They are of *us*, you know.

HASTINGS. But in the company of women of reputation I never saw such an idiot, such a trembler; you look for all the world as if you wanted an opportunity of stealing out of the room.

MARLOW. Why, man, that's because I *do* want to steal out of the room. Faith, I have often formed a resolution to break the ice, and rattle away at any rate. But I don't know how, a single glance from a pair of fine eyes has totally overset my resolution. An impudent fellow may counterfeit modesty, but I'll be hanged if a modest man can ever counterfeit impudence.

HASTINGS. If you could but say half the fine things to them that I have heard you lavish upon the barmaid of an inn, or even a college bed maker—

MARLOW. Why, George, I can't say fine things to them. They freeze, they petrify me. They may talk of a comet, or a burning mountain, or some such bagatelle.[2] But to me, a modest woman, dressed out in all her finery, is the most tremendous object of the whole creation.

HASTINGS. Ha! ha! ha! At this rate, man, how can you ever expect to marry!

MARLOW. Never, unless as among kings and princes, my bride were to be courted by proxy. If, indeed, like an Eastern bridegroom, one were to be introduced to a wife he never saw before, it might be endured. But to go through all the terrors of a formal courtship, together with the episode of aunts, grandmothers and cousins, and at last to blurt out the broad staring question of "Madam, will you marry me?" No, no, that's a strain much above me, I assure you.

HASTINGS. I pity you. But how do you intend behaving to the lady you are come down to visit at the request of your father?

MARLOW. As I behave to all other ladies. Bow very low;

[2] bagatelle trifle

answer yes or no to all her demands. But for the rest, I don't think I shall venture to look in her face, till I see my father's again.

HASTINGS. I'm surprised that one who is so warm a friend can be so cool a lover.

MARLOW. To be explicit, my dear Hastings, my chief inducement down was to be instrumental in forwarding your happiness, not my own. Miss Neville loves you, the family don't know you, as my friend you are sure of a reception, and let honor do the rest.

HASTINGS. My dear Marlow! But I'll suppress the emotion. Were I a wretch, meanly seeking to carry off a fortune, you should be the last man in the world I would apply to for assistance. But Miss Neville's person is all I ask, and that is mine, both from her deceased father's consent, and her own inclination.

MARLOW. Happy man! You have talents and art to captivate any woman. I'm doomed to adore the sex, and yet to converse with the only part of it I despise. This stammer in my address, and this awkward [un]prepossessing visage of mine, can never permit me to soar above the reach of a milliner's 'prentice, or one of the duchesses of Drury Lane.[3] Pshaw! this fellow here to interrupt us.

(*Enter* HARDCASTLE)

HARDCASTLE. Gentlemen, once more you are heartily welcome. Which is Mr. Marlow? Sir, you're heartily welcome. It's not my way, you see, to receive my friends with my back to the fire. I like to give them a hearty reception in the old style at my gate. I like to see their horses and trunks taken care of.

MARLOW. (*Aside*) He has got our names from the servants already. (*To him*) We approve your caution and hospitality, sir. (*To* HASTINGS) I have been thinking, George, of changing our traveling dresses in the morning. I am grown confoundedly ashamed of mine.

HARDCASTLE. I beg, Mr. Marlow, you'll use no ceremony[4] in this house.

HASTINGS. I fancy, Charles, you're right; the first blow

---

[3] duchesses of Drury Lane women of dubious reputation who frequented the Drury Lane district [4] ceremony formality

is half the battle. I intend opening the campaign with the white and gold.

HARDCASTLE. Mr. Marlow—Mr. Hastings—gentlemen, pray be under no restraint in this house. This is Liberty Hall, gentlemen. You may do just as you please here.

MARLOW. Yet, George, if we open the campaign too fiercely at first, we may want ammunition before it is over. I think to reserve the embroidery to secure a retreat.

HARDCASTLE. Your talking of a retreat, Mr. Marlow, puts me in mind of the Duke of Marlborough, when we went to besiege Denain.[5] He first summoned the garrison—

MARLOW. Don't you think the *ventre d'or*[6] waistcoat will do with the plain brown?

HARDCASTLE. He first summoned the garrison, which might consist of about five thousand men—

HASTINGS. I think not: brown and yellow mix but very poorly.

HARDCASTLE. I say, gentlemen, as I was telling you, he summoned the garrison, which might consist of about five thousand men—

MARLOW. The girls like finery.

HARDCASTLE. Which might consist of about five thousand men, well appointed with stores, ammunition, and other implements of war. "Now," says the Duke of Marlborough to George Brooks, that stood next to him—you must have heard of George Brooks—"I'll pawn my dukedom," says he, "but I take that garrison without spilling a drop of blood." So—

MARLOW. What, my good friend, if you gave us a glass of punch in the meantime; it would help us to carry on the siege with vigor.

HARDCASTLE. Punch, sir! (*Aside*) This is the most unaccountable kind of modesty I every met with.

MARLOW. Yes, sir, punch. A glass of warm punch, after our journey, will be comfortable. This is Liberty Hall, you know.

HARDCASTLE. Here's cup,[7] sir.

[5] Denain where the French defeated the Allies under Lord Albemarle in 1712; Marlborough was not present   [6] ventre d'or gold-fronted   [7] cup flavored and sweetened wine, as claret-cup

MARLOW. (*Aside*) So this fellow, in his Liberty Hall, will only let us have just what he pleases.

HARDCASTLE. (*Taking the cup*) I hope you'll find it to your mind. I have prepared it with my own hands, and I believe you'll own the ingredients are tolerable. Will you be so good as to pledge me, sir? Here, Mr. Marlow, here is to our better acquaintance. (*Drinks*)

MARLOW. (*Aside*) A very impudent fellow this! But he's a character, and I'll humor him a little. Sir, my service to you. (*Drinks*)

HASTINGS. (*Aside*) I see this fellow wants to give us his company, and forgets that he's an innkeeper before he has learned to be a gentleman.

MARLOW. From the excellence of your cup, my old friend, I suppose you have a good deal of business in this part of the country. Warm work, now and then, at elections, I suppose.

HARDCASTLE. No, sir, I have long given that work over. Since our betters have hit upon the expedient of electing each other, there is no business "for us that sell ale." [8]

HASTINGS. So, then you have no turn for politics I find.

HARDCASTLE. Not in the least. There was a time, indeed, I fretted myself about the mistakes of government, like other people; but finding myself every day grow more angry, and the government growing no better, I left it to mend itself. Since that, I no more trouble my head about *Heyder Ally,*[9] or *Ally Cawn,*[10] than about *Ally Croaker.*[11] Sir, my service to you.

HASTINGS. So that with eating above stairs, and drinking below, with receiving your friends within, and amusing them without, you lead a good, pleasant, bustling life of it.

HARDCASTLE. I do stir about a great deal, that's certain. Half the differences of the parish are adjusted in this very parlor.

MARLOW. (*After drinking*) And you have an argument

[8] **us that sell ale** refers ambiguously to the free drinks expected by voters from electoral candidates   [9] **Heyder Ally** Hyder Ali, or Haidar Ali, usurper of the throne of Mysore in India, who had defeated the English in 1767   [10] **Ally Cawn** Ally Khan, subahdar of Bengal   [11] **Ally Croaker** the hero of an Irish ballad

in your cup, old gentleman, better than any in Westminster Hall.[12]

HARDCASTLE. Ay, young gentleman, that, and a little philosophy.

MARLOW. (*Aside*) Well, this is the first time I ever heard of an innkeeper's philosophy.

HASTINGS. So then, like an experienced general, you attack them on every quarter. If you find their reason manageable, you attack it with your philosophy; if you find they have no reason, you attack them with this. Here's your health, my philosopher. (*Drinks*)

HARDCASTLE. Good, very good, thank you; ha! ha! Your generalship puts me in mind of Prince Eugene, when he fought the Turks at the battle of Belgrade.[13] You shall hear—

MARLOW. Instead of the battle of Belgrade, I believe it's almost time to talk about supper. What has your philosophy got in the house for supper?

HARDCASTLE. For supper, sir! (*Aside*) Was ever such a request to a man in his own house!

MARLOW. Yes, sir, supper sir; I begin to feel an appetite. I shall make devilish work to-night in the larder, I promise you.

HARDCASTLE. (*Aside*) Such a brazen dog sure never my eyes beheld. (*To him*) Why, really, sir, as for supper, I can't well tell. My Dorothy, and the cook-maid, settle these things between them. I leave these kind of things entirely to them.

MARLOW. You do, do you?

HARDCASTLE. Entirely. By the bye, I believe they are in actual consultation upon what's for supper this moment in the kitchen.

MARLOW. Then I beg they"ll admit *me* as one of their privy council. It's a way I have got. When I travel, I always choose to regulate my own supper. Let the cook be called. No offense I hope, sir.

HARDCASTLE. Oh, no, sir, none in the least; yet I don't know how; our Bridget, the cook-maid, is not very communicative upon these occasions. Should we send for her, she might scold us all out of the house.

[12] Westminster Hall the seat of the law-courts in London
[13] battle of Belgrade won by Prince Eugene in 1717

HASTINGS. Let's see your list of the larder, then. I ask it as a favor. I always match my appetite to my bill of fare.

MARLOW. (*To* HARDCASTLE, *who looks at them with surprise*) Sir, he's very right, and it's my way, too.

HARDCASTLE. Sir, you have a right to command here. Here, Roger, bring us the bill of fare for to-night's supper; I believe it's drawn out. Your manner, Mr. Hastings, puts me in mind of my uncle, Colonel Wallop. It was a saying of his, that no man was sure of his supper till he had eaten it.

HASTINGS. (*Aside*) All upon the high ropes! [14] His uncle a colonel! We shall soon hear of his mother being a justice of peace. But let's hear the bill of fare.

MARLOW. (*Perusing*) What's here? For the first course; for the second course; for the dessert.[15] The devil, sir, do you think we have brought down the whole Joiners' Company,[16] or the Corporation[17] of Bedford, to eat up such a supper? Two or three little things, clean and comfortable, will do.

HASTINGS. But let's hear it.

MARLOW. (*Reading*) "For the first course, at the top, a pig, and prune sauce."

HASTINGS. Damn your pig, I say!

MARLOW. And damn your prune sauce, say I!

HARDCASTLE. And yet, gentlemen, to men that are hungry, pig with prune sauce is very good eating.

MARLOW. "At the bottom, a calf's tongue and brains."

HASTINGS. Let your brains be knocked out, my good sir; I don't like them.

MARLOW. Or you may clap them on a plate by themselves. I do.

HARDCASTLE. (*Aside*) Their impudence confounds me. (*To them*) Gentlemen, you are my guests; make what alterations you please. Is there anything else you wish to retrench or alter, gentlemen?

MARLOW. "Item: a pork pie, a boiled rabbit and sau-

---

[14] **upon the high ropes** pretentious   [15] **first course . . . dessert** the usual procedure at gentlemen's tables was to have two courses of many dishes, with sweets included in the second course; the dessert at the end was fruit   [16] **Joiners' Company** guild of woodworkers   [17] **Corporation** organized merchants

sages, a florentine,[18] a shaking pudding, and a dish of tiff
—taff—taffety[19] cream!"

HASTINGS. Confound your made dishes! [20] I shall be as
much at a loss in this house as at a green and yellow
dinner at the French ambassador's table. I'm for plain
eating.

HARDCASTLE. I'm sorry, gentlemen, that I have nothing
you like; but if there be anything you have a particular
fancy to—

MARLOW. Why, really, sir, your bill of fare is so ex-
quisite, that any one part of it is full as good as another.
Send us what you please. So much for supper. And now
to see that our beds are aired, and properly taken care of.

HARDCASTLE. I entreat you'll leave all that to me. You
shall not stir a step.

MARLOW. Leave that to you! I protest, sir, you must
excuse me; I always look to these things myself.

HARDCASTLE. I must insist, sir, you'll make yourself easy
on that head.

MARLOW. You see I'm resolved on it. (*Aside*) A very
troublesome fellow this, as ever I met with.

HARDCASTLE. Well, sir, I'm resolved at least to attend
you. (*Aside*) This may be modern modesty, but I never
saw anything look so like old-fashioned impudence.

(*Exeunt* MARLOW *and* HARDCASTLE)

HASTINGS. (*Alone*) So I find this fellow's civilities begin
to grow troublesome. But who can be angry at those assiduities which are meant to please him? Ha! what do I
see? Miss Neville, by all that's happy!

(*Enter* MISS NEVILLE)

MISS NEVILLE. My dear Hastings! To what unexpected
good fortune, to what accident, am I to ascribe this happy
meeting?

HASTINGS. Rather let me ask the same question, as I
could never have hoped to meet my dearest Constance at
an inn.

MISS NEVILLE. An inn! sure you mistake! My aunt, my

[18] florentine a deepdish tart made of meat, spices, and currants
[19] taffety taffeta [20] made dishes dishes made of combining
several ingredients, regarded by typical Englishmen as foreign
and unwholesome

guardian, lives here. What could induce you to think **this**
house an inn?

HASTINGS. My friend, Mr. Marlow, with whom I came
down, and I have been sent here as to an inn, I assure
you. A young fellow whom we accidentally met at a house
hard by directed us hither.

MISS NEVILLE. Certainly it must be one of my hopeful
cousin's tricks, of whom you have heard me talk so often;
ha! ha! ha! ha!

HASTINGS. He whom your aunt intends for you? he of
whom I have such just apprehensions?

MISS NEVILLE. You have nothing to fear from him, I
assure you. You'd adore him if you knew how heartily he
despises me. My aunt knows it too, and has undertaken to
court me for him, and actually begins to think she has
made a conquest.

HASTINGS. Thou dear dissembler! You must know, my
Constance, I have just seized this happy opportunity of
my friend's visit here to get admittance into the family.
The horses that carried us down are now fatigued with
their journey, but they'll soon be refreshed; and then, if
my dearest girl will trust in her faithful Hastings, we shall
soon be landed in France, where even among slaves the
laws of marriage are respected.[21]

MISS NEVILLE. I have often told you, that though ready
to obey you, I yet should leave my little fortune behind
with reluctance. The greatest part of it was left me by my
uncle, the India director, and chiefly consists in jewels. I
have been for some time persuading my aunt to let me
wear them. I fancy I'm very near succeeding. The instant
they are put into my possession you shall find me ready to
make them and myself yours.

HASTINGS. Perish the baubles! Your person is all I desire.
In the meantime, my friend Marlow must not be let into
his mistake. I know the strange reserve of his temper is
such, that if abruptly informed of it, he would instantly
quit the house before our plan was ripe for execution.

[21] ever among slaves . . . respected a reference to the un-
popular Marriage Act of 1772 requiring the King's consent to
all royal marriages; the Duke of Gloucester, whose marriage to
Lady Waldegrave had occasioned the law, was present at the
play's first night and received an ovation from the audience at
this point

Miss Neville. But how shall we keep him in the deception? Miss Hardcastle is just returned from walking; what if we still continue to deceive him?—This, this way—
(*They confer*)

(*Enter* Marlow)

Marlow. The assiduities of these good people tease me beyond bearing. My host seems to think it ill manners to leave me alone, and so he claps not only himself but his old-fashioned wife on my back. They talk of coming to sup with us too; and then, I suppose, we are to run the gauntlet through all the rest of the family.—What have we got here?

Hastings. My dear Charles! Let me congratulate you! The most fortunate accident! Who do you think is just alighted?

Marlow. Cannot guess.

Hastings. Our mistresses, boy, Miss Hardcastle and Miss Neville. Give me leave to introduce Miss Constance Neville to your acquaintance. Happening to dine in the neighborhood, they called on their return to take fresh horses here. Miss Hardcastle has just stepped into the next room, and will be back in an instant. Wasn't it lucky? eh!

Marlow. (*Aside*) I have just been mortified enough of all conscience, and here comes something to complete my embarrassment.

Hastings. Well! but wasn't it the most fortunate thing in the world?

Marlow. Oh, yes. Very fortunate—a most joyful encounter— But our dresses, George, you know, are in disorder— What if we should postpone the happiness till to-morrow?—to-morrow at her own house— It will be every bit as convenient—and rather more respectful— To-morrow let it be.   (*Offering to go*)

Hastings. By no means, sir. Your ceremony will displease her. The disorder of your dress will show the ardor of your impatience. Besides, she knows you are in the house, and will permit you to see her.

Marlow. O! the devil! how shall I support it? Hem! hem! Hastings, you must not go. You are to assist me, you know. I shall be confoundedly ridiculous. Yet, hang it, I'll take courage! Hem!

HASTINGS. Pshaw, man! it's but the first plunge, and all's over! She's but a woman, you know.

MARLOW. And of all women, she that I dread most to encounter!

(*Enter* MISS HARDCASTLE, *as returned from walking, a bonnet, etc.*)

HASTINGS. (*Introducing them*) Miss Hardcastle, Mr. Marlow, I'm proud of bringing two persons of such merit together, that only want to know, to esteem each other.

MISS HARDCASTLE. (*Aside*) Now, for meeting my modest gentleman with a demure face, and quite in his own manner. (*After a pause, in which he appears very uneasy and disconcerted*) I'm glad of your safe arrival, sir—I'm told you had some accidents by the way.

MARLOW. Only a few, madam. Yes, we had some. Yes, madam, a good many accidents, but should be sorry— madam—or rather glad of any accidents—that are so agreeably concluded. Hem!

HASTINGS. (*To him*) You never spoke better in your whole life. Keep it up, and I'll insure you the victory.

MISS HARDCASTLE. I'm afraid you flatter, sir. You that have seen so much of the finest company can find little entertainment in an obscure corner of the country.

MARLOW. (*Gathering courage*) I have lived, indeed, in the world, madam; but I have kept very little company. I have been but an observer upon life, madam, while others were enjoying it.

MISS NEVILLE. But that, I am told, is the way to enjoy it at last.

HASTINGS. (*To him*) Cicero never spoke better. Once more, and you are confirmed in assurance forever.

MARLOW. (*To him*) Hem! stand by me then, and when I'm down, throw in a word or two to set me up again.

MISS HARDCASTLE. An observer, like you, upon life, were, I fear, disagreeably employed, since you must have had much more to censure than to approve.

MARLOW. Pardon me, madam. I was always willing to be amused. The folly of most people is rather an object of mirth than uneasiness.

HASTINGS. (*To him*) Bravo, bravo. Never spoke so well in your whole life. Well! Miss Hardcastle, I see that you

and Mr. Marlow are going to be very good company. I
believe our being here will but embarrass the interview.

MARLOW. Not in the least, Mr. Hastings. We like your
company of all things. (*To him*) Zounds! George, sure you
won't go? How can you leave us?

HASTINGS. Our presence will but spoil conversation, so
we'll retire to the next room. (*To him*) You don't consider,
man, that we are to manage a little *tête-à-tête* of our own.

(*Exeunt* HASTINGS *and* MISS NEVILLE)

MISS HARDCASTLE. (*After a pause*) But you have not
been wholly an observer, I presume, sir. The ladies, I
should hope, have employed some part of your addresses.

MARLOW. (*Relapsing into timidity*) Pardon me, madam,
I—I—I—as yet have studied—only—to—deserve them.

MISS HARDCASTLE. And that some say is the very worst
way to obtain them.

MARLOW. Perhaps so, madam. But I love to converse
only with the more grave and sensible part of the sex.—
But I'm afraid I grow tiresome.

MISS HARDCASTLE. Not at all, sir; there is nothing I like
so much as grave conversation myself; I could hear it
forever. Indeed I have often been surprised how a man
of *sentiment* could ever admire those light airy pleasures,
where nothing reaches the heart.

MARLOW. It's—a disease—of the mind, madam. In the
variety of tastes there must be some who, wanting a relish
—for—um—a—um—

MISS HARDCASTLE. I understand you, sir. There must be
some who, wanting a relish for refined pleasures, pretend
to despise what they are incapable of tasting.

MARLOW. My meaning, madam, but infinitely better ex-
pressed. And I can't help observing—a—

MISS HARDCASTLE. (*Aside*) Who could ever suppose this
fellow impudent upon some occasions? (*To him*) You were
going to observe, sir,—

MARLOW. I was observing, madam—I protest, madam,
I forget what I was going to observe.

MISS HARDCASTLE. (*Aside*) I vow and so do I. (*To him*)
You were observing, sir, that in this age of hypocrisy—
something about hypocrisy, sir.

MARLOW. Yes, madam. In this age of hypocrisy there
are few who, upon strict inquiry, do not—a—a—

MISS HARDCASTLE. I understand you perfectly, sir.

MARLOW. (*Aside*) Egad! and that's more than I do myself!

MISS HARDCASTLE. You mean that in this hypocritical age there are few who do not condemn in public what they practice in private, and think they pay every debt to virtue when they praise it.

MARLOW. True, madam; those who have most virtue in their mouths have least of it in their bosoms. But I'm sure I tire you, madam.

MISS HARDCASTLE. Not in the least, sir; there's something so agreeable and spirited in your manner, such life and force—pray, sir, go on.

MARLOW. Yes, madam. I was saying—that there are some occasions—when a total want of courage, madam, destroys all the—and puts us—upon—a—a—a—

MISS HARDCASTLE. I agree with you entirely; a want of courage upon some occasions assumes the appearance of ignorance, and betrays us when we most want to excel. I beg you'll proceed.

MARLOW. Yes, madam. Morally speaking, madam— But I see Miss Neville expecting us in the next room. I would not intrude for the world.

MISS HARDCASTLE. I protest, sir, I never was more agreeably entertained in all my life. Pray go on.

MARLOW. Yes, madam, I was— But she beckons us to join her. Madam, shall I do myself the honor to attend you?

MISS HARDCASTLE. Well, then, I'll follow.

MARLOW. (*Aside*) This pretty smooth dialogue has done for me. (*Exit*)

MISS HARDCASTLE. (*Alone*) Ha! ha! ha! Was there ever such a sober, sentimental interview? I'm certain he scarce looked in my face the whole time. Yet the fellow, but for his unaccountable bashfulness, is pretty well, too. He has good sense, but then so buried in his fears, that it fatigues one more than ignorance. If I could teach him a little confidence, it would be doing somebody that I know of a piece of service. But who is that somebody? That, faith, is a question I can scarce answer. (*Exit*)

(*Enter* TONY *and* MISS NEVILLE, *followed by* MRS. HARDCASTLE *and* HASTINGS)

TONY. What do you follow me for, cousin Con? I wonder you're not ashamed to be so very engaging

MISS NEVILLE. I hope, cousin, one may speak to one's own relations, and not be to blame.

TONY. Ay, but I know what sort of a relation you want to make me though; but it won't do. I tell you, cousin Con, it won't do, so I beg you'll keep your distance. I want no nearer relationship.

(She follows, coquetting him to the back scene)

MRS. HARDCASTLE. Well! I vow, Mr. Hastings, you are very entertaining. There's nothing in the world I love to talk of so much as London, and the fashions, though I was never there myself.

HASTINGS. Never there! You amaze me! From your air and manner, I concluded you had been bred all your life either at Ranelagh,[22] St. James's[23] or Tower Wharf.[24]

MRS. HARDCASTLE. O! sir, you're only pleased to say so. We country persons can have no manner at all. I'm in love with the town, and that serves to raise me above some of our neighboring rustics; but who can have a manner, that has never seen the Pantheon, the Grotto Gardens, the Borough,[25] and such places, where the nobility chiefly resort? All I can do is to enjoy London at secondhand. I take care to know every *tête-à-tête* from the *Scandalous Magazine,* and have all the fashions, as they come out, in a letter from the two Miss Ricketts of Crooked Lane. Pray how do you like this head,[26] Mr. Hastings?

HASTINGS. Extremely elegant and *dégagée,*[27] upon my word, madam. Your friseur[28] is a Frenchman, I suppose?

MRS. HARDCASTLE. I protest I dressed it myself from a print in the *Ladies Memorandum-book* for the last year.

HASTINGS. Indeed! Such a head in a side box, at the playhouse, would draw as many gazers as my Lady Mayoress at a city ball.

---

[22] Ranelagh a fashionable pleasure resort in Chelsea, near London [23] St. James's the royal palace of St. James in London [24] Tower Wharf in the most plebeian quarter of London [25] the Pantheon . . . the Borough Mrs. Hardcastle here shows her social ignorance by putting on a par the fashionable Pantheon, recently opened on Oxford Street, and the vulgar Grotto Gardens in the Borough of Southwark [26] head headdress [27] dégagée graceful [28] friseur hairdresser

MRS. HARDCASTLE. I vow, since inoculation[29] began, there is no such thing to be seen as a plain woman; so one must dress a little particular or one may escape in the crowd.

HASTINGS. But that can never be your case, madam, in any dress. (*Bowing*)

MRS. HARDCASTLE. Yet, what signifies *my* dressing, when I have such a piece of antiquity by my side as Mr. Hardcastle? All I can say will never argue down a single button from his clothes. I have often wanted him to throw off his great flaxen wig[30] and where he was bald to plaster it over, like my Lord Pately, with powder.

HASTINGS. You are right, madam; for, as among the ladies there are none ugly, so among the men there are none old.

MRS. HARDCASTLE. But what do you think his answer was? Why, with his usual Gothic[31] vivacity, he said I only wanted him to throw off his wig to convert it into a *tête*[32] for my own wearing.

HASTINGS. Intolerable! At your age you may wear what you please, and it must become you.

MRS. HARDCASTLE. Pray, Mr. Hastings, what do you take to be the most fashionable age about town?

HASTINGS. Some time ago, forty was all the mode; but I'm told the ladies intend to bring up fifty for the ensuing winter.

MRS. HARDCASTLE. Seriously? Then I shall be too young for the fashion.

HASTINGS. No lady begins now to put on jewels till she's past forty. For instance, Miss there, in a polite circle, would be considered as a child, as a mere maker of samplers.

MRS. HARDCASTLE. And yet, Mrs. Niece thinks herself as much a woman, and is as fond of jewels, as the oldest of us all.

HASTINGS. Your niece, is she? And that young gentleman, a brother of yours, I should presume?

---

[29] **inoculation** the forerunner of Jenner's vaccination against smallpox, introduced from Turkey by Lady Mary Wortley Montagu in 1721   [30] **flaxen wig** the elaborate wig was going out of fashion, and in its place men of mode were adopting an arrangement of the natural hair stiffened with pomatum and powdered white   [31] **Gothic** uncouth   [32] **tête** headdress

MRS. HARDCASTLE. My son, sir. They are contracted to each other. Observe their little sports. They fall in and out ten times a day, as if they were man and wife already. (*To them*) Well, Tony, child, what soft things are you saying to your cousin Constance this evening?

TONY. I have been saying no soft things; but that it's very hard to be followed about so. Ecod! I've not a place in the house now that's left to myself but the stable.

MRS. HARDCASTLE. Never mind him, Con, my dear. He's in another story behind your back.

MISS NEVILLE. There's something generous in my cousin's manner. He falls out before faces to be forgiven in private.

TONY. That's a damned confounded—crack.

MRS. HARDCASTLE. Ah, he's a sly one! Don't you think they're like each other about the mouth, Mr. Hastings? The Blenkinsop mouth to a T. They're of a size, too. Back to back, my pretties, that Mr. Hastings may see you. Come, Tony.

TONY. You had as good not make me, I tell you.
(*Measuring*)

MISS NEVILLE. O lud! he has almost cracked my head.

MRS. HARDCASTLE. O the monster! For shame, Tony. You a man, and behave so!

TONY. If I'm a man, let me have my fortin. Ecod! I'll not be made a fool of no longer.

MRS. HARDCASTLE. Is this, ungrateful boy, all that I'm to get for the pains I have taken in your education? I that have rocked you in your cradle, and fed that pretty mouth with a spoon! Did not I work that waistcoat to make you genteel? Did not I prescribe for you every day, and weep while the receipt was operating?

TONY. Ecod! you had reason to weep, for you have been dosing me ever since I was born. I have gone through every receipt in *The Complete Huswife*[33] ten times over; and you have thoughts of coursing me through *Quincy*[34] next spring. But, ecod! I tell you, I'll not be made a fool of no longer.

---

[33] **Complete Huswife** a popular handbook of medicine for home-dosing, which was customary in eighteenth-century households
[34] **Quincy** Dr. John Quincy's *Complete English Dispensatory*, first published in 1714, and in its fourteenth edition by 1774

MRS. HARDCASTLE. Wasn't it all for your good, viper? Wasn't it all for your good?

TONY. I wish you'd let me and my good alone, then. Snubbing this way when I'm in spirits! If I'm to have any good, let it come of itself; not to keep dinging it, dinging it into one so.

MRS. HARDCASTLE. That's false; I never see you when you're in spirits. No, Tony, you then go to the alehouse or kennel. I'm never to be delighted with your agreeable wild notes, unfeeling monster!

TONY. Ecod! mamma, your own notes are the wildest of the two.

MRS. HARDCASTLE. Was ever the like? But I see he wants to break my heart, I see he does.

HASTINGS. Dear madam, permit me to lecture the young gentleman a little. I'm certain I can persuade him to his duty.

MRS. HARDCASTLE. Well! I must retire. Come, Constance, my love. You see, Mr. Hastings, the wretchedness of my situation. Was ever poor woman so plagued with a dear, sweet, pretty, provoking, undutiful boy?

(*Exeunt* MRS. HARDCASTLE *and* MISS NEVILLE)

TONY. (*Singing*) *There was a young man riding by, and fain would have his will. Rang do didlo dee.* Don't mind her. Let her cry. It's the comfort of her heart. I have seen her and sister cry over a book[35] for an hour together, and they said they liked the book the better the more it made them cry.

HASTINGS. Then you're no friend to the ladies, I find, my pretty young gentleman?

TONY. That's as I find 'um.

HASTINGS. Not to her of your mother's choosing, I dare answer? And yet she appears to me a pretty, well-tempered girl.

TONY. That's because you don't know her as well as I. Ecod! I know every inch about her; and there's not a more bitter cantankerous toad in all Christendom.

HASTINGS. (*Aside*) Pretty encouragement this for a lover!

TONY. I have seen her since the height of that. She has

---

[35] **cry over a book** obviously a sentimental novel.

as many tricks as a hare in a thicket, or a colt the first day's breaking.

HASTINGS. To me she appears sensible and silent!

TONY. Ay, before company. But when she's with her playmates, she's as loud as a hog in a gate.

HASTINGS. But there is a meek modesty about her that charms me.

TONY. Yes, but curb her never so little, she kicks up, and you're flung in a ditch.

HASTINGS. Well, but you must allow her a little beauty.—Yes, you must allow her some beauty.

TONY. Bandbox![36] She's all a made-up thing, mun. Ah! could you but see Bet Bouncer of these parts, you might then talk of beauty. Ecod, she has two eyes as black as sloes,[37] and cheeks as broad and red as a pulpit cushion. She'd make two of she.

HASTINGS. Well, what say you to a friend that would take this bitter bargain off your hands?

TONY. Anon.[38]

HASTINGS. Would you thank him that would take Miss Neville and leave you to happiness and your dear Betsy?

TONY. Ay; but where is there such a friend, for who would take *her*?

HASTINGS. I am he. If you but assist me, I'll engage to whip her off to France, and you shall never hear more of her.

TONY. Assist you! Ecod I will, to the last drop of my blood. I'll clap a pair of horses to your chaise that shall trundle you off in a twinkling, and maybe get you a part of her fortin besides, in jewels, that you little dream of.

HASTINGS. My dear Squire, this looks like a lad of spirit.

TONY. Come along then, and you shall see more of my spirit before you have done with me. (*Singing*)

> *We are the boys*
> *That fears no noise*
> *Where the thundering cannons roar.* (*Exeunt*)

---

[36] **Bandbox** something light and valueless enough to be carried in a bandbox [37] **sloes** the plums of the sloe or blackthorn [38] **Anon** say it again

Act III

❧

SCENE. *The House*

(*Enter* HARDCASTLE)

HARDCASTLE. What could my old friend Sir Charles mean by recommending his son as the modestest young man in town? To me he appears the most impudent piece of brass that ever spoke with a tongue. He has taken possession of the easy-chair by the fireside already. He took off his boots in the parlor, and desired me to see them taken care of. I'm desirious to know how his impudence affects my daughter.—She will certainly be shocked at it.

(*Enter* MISS HARDCASTLE, *plainly dressed*)

HARDCASTLE. Well, my Kate, I see you have changed your dress, as I bid you; and yet, I believe, there was no great occasion.

MISS HARDCASTLE. I find such a pleasure, sir, in obeying your commands, that I take care to observe them without ever debating their propriety.

HARDCASTLE. And yet, Kate, I sometimes give you some cause, particularly when I recommended my *modest* gentleman to you as a lover to-day.

MISS HARDCASTLE. You taught me to expect something extraordinary, and I find the original exceeds the description.

HARDCASTLE. I was never so surprised in my life! He has quite confounded all my faculties!

MISS HARDCASTLE. I never saw anything like it; and a man of the world, too!

HARDCASTLE. Ay, he learned it all abroad,—what a fool was I, to think a young man could learn modesty by traveling. He might as soon learn wit at a masquerade.

MISS HARDCASTLE. It seems all natural to him.

HARDCASTLE. A good deal assisted by bad company and a French dancing master.

MISS HARDCASTLE. Sure, you mistake, papa! A French dancing master could never have taught him that timid look—that awkward address—that bashful manner—

HARDCASTLE. Whose look, whose manner, child?

MISS HARDCASTLE. Mr. Marlow's: his *mauvaise honte*,[1] his timidity, struck me at the first sight.

HARDCASTLE. Then your first sight deceived you; for I think him one of the most brazen first sights that ever astonished my senses.

MISS HARDCASTLE. Sure, sir, you rally![2] I never saw anyone so modest.

HARDCASTLE. And can you be serious! I never saw such a bouncing swaggering puppy since I was born. Bully Dawson[3] was but a fool to him.

MISS HARDCASTLE. Surprising! He met me with a respectful bow, a stammering voice, and a look fixed on the ground.

HARDCASTLE. He met me with a loud voice, a lordly air, and a familiarity that made my blood freeze again.

MISS HARDCASTLE. He treated me with diffidence and respect; censured the manners of the age; admired the prudence of girls that never laughed; tired me with apologies for being tiresome; then left the room with a bow, and "Madam, I would not for the world detain you."

HARDCASTLE. He spoke to me as if he knew me all his life before. Asked twenty questions, and never waited for an answer. Interrupted my best remarks with some silly pun; and when I was in my best story of the Duke of Marlborough and Prince Eugene, he asked if I had not a good hand at making punch. Yes, Kate, he asked your father if he was a maker of punch!

MISS HARDCASTLE. One of us must certainly be mistaken.

HARDCASTLE. If he be what he has shown himself, I'm determined he shall never have my consent.

MISS HARDCASTLE. And if he be the sullen thing I take him, he shall never have mine.

HARDCASTLE. In one thing then we are agreed—to reject him.

MISS HARDCASTLE. Yes. But upon conditions. For if you should find him less impudent, and I more presuming; if

[1] **mauvaise honte** shamefacedness   [2] **rally** jest   [3] **Bully Dawson** a notorious rascal of the seventeenth century

you find him more respectful, and I more importunate—I don't know—the fellow is well enough for a man— Certainly we don't meet many such at a horse race in the country.

HARDCASTLE. If we should find him so— But that's impossible. The first appearance has done my business. I'm seldom deceived in that.

MISS HARDCASTLE. And yet there may be many good qualities under that first appearance.

HARDCASTLE. Ay, when a girl finds a fellow's outside to her taste, she then sets about guessing the rest of his furniture. With her, a smooth face stands for good sense, and a genteel figure for every virtue.

MISS HARDCASTLE. I hope, sir, a conversation begun with a compliment to my good sense won't end with a sneer at my understanding?

HARDCASTLE. Pardon me, Kate. But if young Mr. Brazen can find the art of reconciling contradictions, he may please us both, perhaps.

MISS HARDCASTLE. And as one of us must be mistaken, what if we go to make further discoveries?

HARDCASTLE. Agreed. But depend on 't, I'm in the right.

MISS HARDCASTLE. And, depend on 't, I'm not much in the wrong. (*Exeunt*)

(*Enter* TONY, *running in with a casket*)

TONY. Ecod! I have got them. Here they are. My cousin Con's necklaces, bobs[4] and all. My mother shan't cheat the poor souls out their fortune neither. O! my genus, is that you?

(*Enter* HASTINGS)

HASTINGS. My dear friend, how have you managed with your mother? I hope you have amused her with pretending love for your cousin, and that you are willing to be reconciled at last? Our horses will be refreshed in a short time, and we shall soon be ready to set off.

TONY. And here's something to bear your charges by the way—(*giving the casket*) your sweetheart's jewels. Keep them, and hang those, I say, that would rob you of one of them.

⁴ **bobs** pendants

HASTINGS. But how have you procured them from your mother?

TONY. Ask me no questions, and I'll tell you no fibs. I procured them by the rule of thumb. If I had not a key to every drawer in my mother's bureau, how could I go to the alehouse so often as I do? An honest man may rob himself of his own at any time.

HASTINGS. Thousands do it every day. But, to be plain with you, Miss Neville is endeavoring to procure them from her aunt this very instant. If she succeeds, it will be the most delicate way, at least, of obtaining them.

TONY. Well, keep them, till you know how it will be. But I know how it will be well enough; she'd as soon part with the only sound tooth in her head.

HASTINGS. But I dread the effects of her resentment, when she finds she has lost them.

TONY. Never you mind her resentment; leave *me* to manage that. I don't value her resentment the bounce of a cracker. Zounds! here they are! Morrice! [5] Prance!

(Exit HASTINGS*)*

(Enter MRS. HARDCASTLE *and* MISS NEVILLE*)*

MRS. HARDCASTLE. Indeed, Constance, you amaze me. Such a girl as you want jewels? It will be time enough for jewels, my dear, twenty years hence, when your beauty begins to want repairs.

MISS NEVILLE. But what will repair beauty at forty will certainly improve it at twenty, madam.

MRS. HARDCASTLE. Yours, my dear, can admit of none. That natural blush is beyond a thousand ornaments. Besides, child, jewels are quite out at present. Don't you see half the ladies of our acquaintance, my Lady Kill-day-light, and Mrs. Crump, and the rest of them, carry their jewels to town, and bring nothing but paste and marcasites[6] back?

MISS NEVILLE. But who knows, madam, but somebody that shall be nameless would like me best with all my little finery about me?

MRS. HARDCASTLE. Consult your glass, my dear, and then see, if with such a pair of eyes, you want any better sparklers. What do you think, Tony, my dear? Does your

[5] Morrice do a Morris dance   [6] marcasites ornaments made of marcasite, or iron pyrites, a cheap substitute for gold or silver

cousin Con want any jewels, in your eyes, to set off her beauty?

TONY. That's as thereafter may be.

MISS NEVILLE. My dear aunt, if you knew how it would oblige me.

MRS. HARDCASTLE. A parcel of old-fashioned rose and table-cut[7] things. They would make you look like the court of King Solomon at a puppet show. Besides, I believe I can't readily come at them. They may be missing for aught I know to the contrary.

TONY. (*Apart to* MRS. HARDCASTLE) Then why don't you tell her so at once, as she's so longing for them? Tell her they're lost. It's the only way to quiet her. Say they're lost, and call me to bear witness.

MRS. HARDCASTLE. (*Apart to* TONY) You know, my dear, I'm only keeping them for you. So if I say they're gone, you'll bear me witness, will you? He! he! he!

TONY. Never fear me. Ecod! I'll say I saw them taken out with my own eyes.

MISS NEVILLE. I desire them but for a day, madam; just to be permitted to show them as relics, and then they may be locked up again.

MRS. HARDCASTLE. To be plain with you, my dear Constance, if I could find them you should have them. They're missing, I assure you. Lost, for aught I know; but we must have patience, wherever they are.

MISS NEVILLE. I'll not believe it; this is but a shallow pretense to deny me. I know they're too valuable to be so slightly kept, and as you are to answer for the loss—

MRS. HARDCASTLE. Don't be alarmed, Constance. If they be lost, I must restore an equivalent. But my son knows they are missing, and not to be found.

TONY. That I can bear witness to. They are missing, and not to be found; I'll take my oath on't.

MRS. HARDCASTLE. You must learn resignation, my dear; for though we lose our fortune, yet we should not lose our patience. See me, how calm I am.

MISS NEVILLE. Ay, people are generally calm at the misfortunes of others.

[7] **rose and table-cut** two modes of gem cutting usually employed for stones of lesser value, the largest and finest ones being **brilliant-cut**

MRS. HARDCASTLE. Now, I wonder a girl of your good sense should waste a thought upon such trumpery. We shall soon find them; and, in the meantime, you shall make use of my garnets till your jewels be found.

MISS NEVILLE. I detest garnets.

MRS. HARDCASTLE. The most becoming things in the world to set off a clear complexion. You have often seen how well they look upon me. You *shall* have them.

(*Exit*)

MISS NEVILLE. I dislike them of all things. You shan't stir.—Was ever anything so provoking to mislay my own jewels, and force me to wear her trumpery?

TONY. Don't be a fool. If she gives you the garnets, take what you can get. The jewels are your own already. I have stolen them out of her bureau, and she does not know it. Fly to your spark; he'll tell you more of the matter. Leave me to manage *her*.

MISS NEVILLE. My dear cousin!

TONY. Vanish. She's here, and has missed them already.

(*Exit* MISS NEVILLE)

Zounds! how she fidgets and spits about like a Catherine wheel.

(*Enter* MRS. HARDCASTLE)

MRS. HARDCASTLE. Confusion! thieves! robbers! we are cheated, plundered, broke open, undone!

TONY. What's the matter, what's the matter, mamma? I hope nothing has happened to any of the good family?

MRS. HARDCASTLE. We are robbed. My bureau has been broke open, the jewels taken out, and I'm undone!

TONY. Oh! is that all! Ha! ha! ha! By the laws, I never saw it better acted in my life. Ecod, I thought you was ruined in earnest, ha, ha, ha!

MRS. HARDCASTLE. Why, boy, I *am* ruined in earnest. My bureau has been broke open, and all taken away.

TONY. Stick to that; ha, ha, ha! stick to that. I'll bear witness, you know! call me to bear witness.

MRS. HARDCASTLE. I tell you, Tony, by all that's precious, the jewels are gone, and I shall be ruined forever.

TONY. Sure I know they're gone, and I am to say so.

MRS. HARDCASTLE. My dearest Tony, but hear me. They're gone, I say.

TONY. By the laws, mamma, you make me for to laugh, ha! ha! I know who took them well enough, ha! ha! ha!

MRS. HARDCASTLE. Was there ever such a blockhead, that can't tell the difference between jest and earnest? I tell you I'm not in jest, booby.

TONY. That's right, that's right! You must be in a bitter passion, and then nobody will suspect either of us. I'll bear witness that they are gone.

MRS. HARDCASTLE. Was there ever such a cross-grained brute, that won't hear me! Can you bear witness that you're no better than a fool? Was ever poor woman so beset with fools on one hand, and thieves on the other?

TONY. I can bear witness to that.

MRS. HARDCASTLE. Bear witness again, you blockhead you, and I'll turn you out of the room directly. My poor niece, what will become of *her?* Do you laugh, you unfeeling brute, as if you enjoyed my distress?

TONY. I can bear witness to that.

MRS. HARDCASTLE. Do you insult me, monster? I'll teach you to vex your mother, I will!

TONY. I can bear witness to that.

(He runs off; she follows him)

(Enter MISS HARDCASTLE *and* MAID)

MISS HARDCASTLE. What an unaccountable creature is that brother of mine, to send them to the house as an inn, ha! ha! I don't wonder at his impudence.

MAID. But what is more, madam, the young gentleman, as you passed by in your present dress, asked me if you were the barmaid. He mistook you for the barmaid, madam.

MISS HARDCASTLE. Did he? then as I live I'm resolved to keep up the delusion. Tell me, Pimple, how do you like my present dress? Don't you think I look something like Cherry[8] in the *Beaux' Stratagem?*

MAID. It's the dress, madam, that every lady wears in the country, but when she visits or receives company.

---

[8] **Cherry** the innkeeper's daughter in Farquhar's comedy *The Beaux' Stratagem* (1707); Goldsmith admired Farquhar because he introduced common-life characters and lively action into the restricted social world of Restoration comedy

MISS HARDCASTLE. And are you sure he does not remember my face or person?

MAID. Certain of it.

MISS HARDCASTLE. I vow I thought so; for though we spoke for some time together, yet his fears were such that he never once looked up during the interview. Indeed, if he had, my bonnet would have kept him from seeing me.

MAID. But what do you hope from keeping him in his mistake?

MISS HARDCASTLE. In the first place, I shall be *seen*, and that is no small advantage to a girl who brings her face to market. Then I shall perhaps make an acquaintance, and that's no small victory gained over one who never addresses any but the wildest of her sex. But my chief aim is to take my gentleman off his guard, and like an invisible champion of romance examine the giant's force before I offer to combat.

MAID. But are you sure you can act your part, and disguise your voice so that he may mistake that, as he has already mistaken your person?

MISS HARDCASTLE. Never fear me. I think I have got the true bar cant[9]— Did your honor call?—Attend the Lion there.—Pipes and tobacco for the Angel.—The Lamb[10] has been outrageous this half hour.

MAID. It will do, madam. But he's here.   (*Exit* MAID)

(*Enter* MARLOW)

MARLOW. What a bawling in every part of the house; I have scarce a moment's repose. If I go to the best room, there I find my host and his story. If I fly to the gallery, there we have my hostess with her curtsy down to the ground. I have at last got a moment to myself, and now for recollection. (*Walks and muses*)

MISS HARDCASTLE. Did you call, sir? Did your honor call?

MARLOW. (*Musing*) As for Miss Hardcastle, she's too grave and sentimental for me.

MISS HARDCASTLE. Did your honor call? (*She still places herself before him, he turning away*)

[9] cant lingo   [10] Lion . . . Lamb oldfashioned inns still named their rooms, as in Shakespeare's day

MARLOW. No, child. (*Musing*) Besides, from the glimpse I had of her, I think she squints.

MISS HARDCASTLE. I'm sure, sir, I heard the bell ring.

MARLOW. No, no. (*Musing*) I have pleased my father, however, by coming down, and I'll to-morrow please myself by returning. (*Taking out his tablets*[11] *and perusing*)

MISS HARDCASTLE. Perhaps the other gentleman called, sir?

MARLOW. I tell you no.

MISS HARDCASTLE. I should be glad to know, sir. We have such a parcel of servants.

MARLOW. No, no, I tell you. (*Looks full in her face*) Yes, child, I think I did call. I wanted—I wanted—I vow, child, you are vastly handsome.

MISS HARDCASTLE. O, la, sir, you'll make one ashamed.

MARLOW. Never saw a more sprightly, malicious eye. Yes, yes, my dear, I did call. Have you got any of your—a—what d'ye call it in the house?

MISS HARDCASTLE. No, sir, we have been out of that these ten days.

MARLOW. One may call in this house, I find, to very little purpose. Suppose I should call for a taste, just by way of trial, of the nectar of your lips; perhaps I might be disappointed in that too.

MISS HARDCASTLE. Nectar! nectar! That's a liquor there's no call for in these parts. French, I suppose. We keep no French wines here, sir.

MARLOW. Of true English growth, I assure you.

MISS HARDCASTLE. Then it's odd I should not know it. We brew all sorts of wines in this house, and I have lived here these eighteen years.

MARLOW. Eighteen years! Why, one would think, child, you kept the bar before you were born. How old are you?

MISS HARDCASTLE. O! sir, I must not tell my age. They say women and music should never be dated.

MARLOW. To guess at this distance, you can't be much above forty. (*Approaching*) Yet nearer, I don't think so much. (*Approaching*) By coming close to some women, they look younger still; but when we come very close indeed—(*Attempting to kiss her*)

MISS HARDCASTLE. Pray, sir, keep your distance. One
[11] **tablets** memorandum book

would think you wanted to know one's age as they do horses, by mark of mouth.

MARLOW. I protest, child, you use me extremely ill. If you keep me at this distance, how is it possible you and I can be ever acquainted?

MISS HARDCASTLE. And who wants to be acquainted with you? I want no such acquaintance, not I. I'm sure you did not treat Miss Hardcastle, that was here a while ago, in this obstropalous[12] manner. I'll warrant me, before her you looked dashed, and kept bowing to the ground, and talked, for all the world, as if you was before a justice of peace.

MARLOW. (*Aside*) Egad! she has hit it, sure enough. (*To her*) In awe of her, child? Ha! ha! ha! A mere awkward, squinting thing! No, no. I find you don't know me. I laughed, and rallied [13] her a little; but I was unwilling to be too severe. No, I could not be too severe, *curse me!*

MISS HARDCASTLE. O! then, sir, you are a favorite, I find, among the ladies?

MARLOW. Yes, my dear, a great favorite. And yet, hang me, I don't see what they find in me to follow. At the Ladies' Club in town I'm called their agreeable Rattle. Rattle, child, is not my real name, but one I'm known by. My name is Solomons. Mr. Solomons, my dear, at your service. (*Offering to salute[14] her*)

MISS HARDCASTLE. Hold, sir; you are introducing me to your club, not to yourself. And you're so great a favorite there, you say?

MARLOW. Yes, my dear. There's Mrs. Mantrap, Lady Betty Blackleg, the Countess of Sligo, Mrs. Langhorns, old Miss Biddy Buckskin,[15] and your humble servant, keep up the spirit of the place.

MISS HARDCASTLE. Then it's a very merry place, I suppose.

MARLOW. Yes, as merry as cards, suppers, wine, and old women can make us.

---

[12] **obstropalous** a barmaid version of "obstreperous"   [13] **rallied** teased   [14] **salute** kiss   [15] **Biddy Buckskin** originally "Rachel Buckskin" but altered after the first night because Miss Rachel Lloyd, moving spirit in the fashionable Albemarle Street Club, resented it as an allusion to herself

MISS HARDCASTLE. And their agreeable Rattle, ha! ha! ha!

MARLOW. (*Aside*) Egad! I don't quite like this chit. She looks knowing, methinks. You laugh, child?

MISS HARDCASTLE. I can't but laugh to think what time they all have for minding their work, or their family.

MARLOW. (*Aside*) All's well; she don't laugh at me. (*To her*) Do *you* ever work, child?

MISS HARDCASTLE. Ay, sure. There's not a screen or a quilt in the whole house but what can bear witness to that.

MARLOW. Odso! then you must show me your embroidery. I embroider and draw patterns myself a little. If you want a judge of your work, you must apply to me. (*Seizing her hand*)

(*Enter* HARDCASTLE, *who stands in surprise*)

MISS HARDCASTLE. Ay, but the colors don't look well by candlelight. You shall see all in the morning. (*Struggling*)

MARLOW. And why not now, my angel? Such beauty fires beyond the power of resistance.—Pshaw! the father here! My old luck; I never nicked seven that I did not throw ames ace[16] three times following. (*Exit* MARLOW)

HARDCASTLE. So. Madam! So I find *this* is your *modest* lover. This is your humble admirer, that kept his eyes fixed on the ground, and only adored at humble distance. Kate, Kate, art thou not ashamed to deceive your father so?

MISS HARDCASTLE. Never trust me, dear papa, but he's still the modest man I first took him for; you'll be convinced of it as well as I.

HARDCASTLE. By the hand of my body, I believe his impudence is infectious! Didn't I see him seize your hand? Didn't I see him haul you about like a milkmaid? And now you talk of his respect and his modesty, forsooth!

MISS HARDCASTLE. But if I shortly convince you of his modesty, that he has only the faults that will pass off

[16] **nicked seven . . . ames ace** terms used in dicing; Marlow means "If I get one lucky throw I then get three unlucky ones to offset it" (ames ace, or ambsace, means double-ace, and was of course the lowest possible throw)

with time, and the virtues that will improve with age, I hope you'll forgive him.

HARDCASTLE. The girl would actually make one run mad! I tell you I'll not be convinced. I am convinced. He has scarcely been three hours in the house, and he has already encroached on all my prerogatives. You may like his impudence, and call it modesty; but my son-in-law, madam, must have very different qualifications.

MISS HARDCASTLE. Sir, I ask but this night to convince you.

HARDCASTLE. You shall not have half the time, for I have thoughts of turning him out this very hour.

MISS HARDCASTLE. Give me that hour, then, and I hope to satisfy you.

HARDCASTLE. Well, an hour let it be then. But I'll have no trifling with your father. All fair and open, do you mind me?

MISS HARDCASTLE. I hope, sir, you have ever found that I considered your commands as my pride; for your kindness is such, that my duty as yet has been inclination.

(*Exeunt*)

Act IV

❦

SCENE. *The House*

(*Enter* HASTINGS *and* MISS NEVILLE)

HASTINGS. You surprise me! Sir Charles Marlow expected here this night? Where have you had your information?

MISS NEVILLE. You may depend upon it. I just saw his letter to Mr. Hardcastle, in which he tells him he intends setting out a few hours after his son.

HASTINGS. Then, my Constance, all must be completed before he arrives. He knows me; and should he find me here, would discover my name, and perhaps my designs, to the rest of the family.

MISS NEVILLE. The jewels, I hope, are safe.

HASTINGS. Yes, yes. I have sent them to Marlow, who keeps the keys of our baggage. In the meantime, I'll go to prepare matters for our elopement. I have had the Squire's promise of a fresh pair of horses; and, if I should not see him again, will write him further directions.

(Exit)

MISS NEVILLE. Well! success attend you. In the meantime, I'll go amuse my aunt with the old pretense of a violent passion for my cousin. *(Exit)*

(Enter MARLOW, *followed by a* SERVANT)

MARLOW. I wonder what Hastings could mean by sending me so valuable a thing as a casket to keep for him, when he knows the only place I have is the seat of a post coach at an inn door. Have you deposited the casket with the landlady, as I ordered you? Have you put it into her own hands?

SERVANT. Yes, your honor.

MARLOW. She said she'd keep it safe, did she?

SERVANT. Yes; she said she'd keep it safe enough; she asked me how I came by it; and she said she had a great mind to make me give an account of myself.

(Exit SERVANT)

MARLOW. Ha! ha! ha! They're safe, however. What an unaccountable set of beings have we got amongst! This little barmaid, though, runs in my head most strangely, and drives out the absurdities of all the rest of the family. She's mine, she must be mine, or I'm greatly mistaken.

(Enter HASTINGS)

HASTINGS. Bless me! I quite forgot to tell her that I intended to prepare at the bottom of the garden. Marlow here, and in spirits too!

MARLOW. Give me joy, George! Crown me, shadow me with laurels! Well, George, after all, we modest fellows don't want for success among the women.

HASTINGS. Some women, you mean. But what success has your honor's modesty been crowned with now, that it grows so insolent upon us?

MARLOW. Didn't you see the tempting, brisk, lovely little thing, that runs about the house with a bunch of keys to its girdle?

HASTINGS. Well! and what then?

MARLOW. She's mine, you rogue, you. Such fire, such motion, such eyes, such lips—but, egad! she would not let me kiss them though.

HASTINGS. But are you so sure, so very sure of her?

MARLOW. Why, man, she talked of showing me her work abovestairs, and I am to improve the pattern.

HASTINGS. But how can *you*, Charles, go about to rob a woman of her honor?

MARLOW. Pshaw! pshaw! We all know the honor of the barmaid of an inn. I don't intend to *rob* her, take my word for it; there's nothing in this house I shan't honestly *pay* for.

HASTINGS. I believe the girl has virtue.

MARLOW. And if she has, I should be the last man in the world that would attempt to corrupt it.

HASTINGS. You have taken care, I hope, of the casket I sent you to lock up? It's in safety?

MARLOW. Yes, yes. It's safe enough. I have taken care of it. But how could you think the seat of a post coach at an inn door a place of safety? Ah! numskull! I have taken better precautions for you than you did for yourself— I have—

HASTINGS. What?

MARLOW. I have sent it to the landlady to keep for you.

HASTINGS. To the landlady!

MARLOW. The landlady.

HASTINGS. You did?

MARLOW. I did. She's to be answerable for its forthcoming, you know.

HASTINGS. Yes, she'll bring it forth, with a witness.

MARLOW. Wasn't I right? I believe you'll allow that I acted prudently upon this occasion?

HASTINGS. (*Aside*) He must not see my uneasiness.

MARLOW. You seem a little disconcerted though, methinks. Sure nothing has happened?

HASTINGS. No, nothing. Never was in better spirits in all my life. And so you left it with the landlady, who, no doubt, very readily undertook the charge?

MARLOW. Rather too readily. For she not only kept the casket, but, through her great precaution, was going to keep the messenger too. Ha! ha! ha!

HASTINGS. He! he! he! They're safe however.

MARLOW. As a guinea in a miser's purse.

HASTINGS. (*Aside*) So now all hopes of fortune are at an end, and we must set off without it. (*To him*) Well, Charles, I'll leave you to your meditations on the pretty barmaid, and, he! he! he! may you be as successful for yourself as you have been for me.   (*Exit*)

MARLOW. Thank ye, George! I ask no more. Ha! ha! ha!

(*Enter* HARDCASTLE)

HARDCASTLE. I no longer know my own house. It's turned all topsy-turvy. His servants have got drunk already. I'll bear it no longer; and yet, from my respect for his father, I'll be calm. (*To him*) Mr. Marlow, your servant. I'm your very humble servant. (*Bowing low*)

MARLOW. Sir, your humble servant. (*Aside*) What's to be the wonder now?

HARDCASTLE. I believe, sir, you must be sensible, sir, that no man alive ought to be more welcome than your father's son, sir. I hope you think so?

MARLOW. I do from my soul, sir. I don't want much intreaty. I generally make my father's son welcome wherever he goes.

HARDCASTLE. I believe you do, from my soul, sir. But though I say nothing to your own conduct, that of your servants is insufferable. Their manner of drinking is setting a very bad example in this house, I assure you.

MARLOW. I protest, my very good sir, that's no fault of mine. If they don't drink as they ought, *they* are to blame. I ordered them not to spare the cellar. I did, I assure you. (*To the side scene*) Here, let one of my servants come up. (*To him*) My positive directions were, that as I did not drink myself, they should make up for my deficiencies below.

HARDCASTLE. Then they had your orders for what they do! I'm satisfied!

MARLOW. They had, I assure you. You shall hear from one of themselves.

(Enter Servant, *drunk)*

Marlow. You, Jeremy! Come forward, sirrah! What were my orders? Were you not told to drink freely, and call for what you thought fit, for the good of the house?

Hardcastle. *(Aside)* I begin to lose my patience.

Jeremy. Please your honor, liberty and Fleet Street[1] forever! Though I'm but a servant, I'm as good as another man. I'll drink for no man before supper, sir, dammy! Good liquor will sit upon a good supper, but a good supper will not sit upon—hiccup—upon my conscience, sir.

(Exit)

Marlow. You see, my old friend, the fellow is as drunk as he can possibly be. I don't know what you'd have more, unless you'd have the poor devil soused in a beer barrel.

Hardcastle. Zounds! he'll drive me distracted if I contain my self any longer. Mr. Marlow, sir! I have submitted to your insolence for more than four hours, and I see no likelihood of its coming to an end. I'm now resolved to be master here, sir, and I desire that you and your drunken pack may leave my house directly.

Marlow. Leave your house!—Sure you jest, my good friend? What? when I am doing what I can to please you!

Hardcastle. I tell you, sir, you don't please me; so I desire you'll leave my house.

Marlow. Sure you cannot be serious? At this time o' night, and such a night. You only mean to banter[2] me?

Hardcastle. I tell you, sir, I'm serious; and now that my passions are roused, I say this house is mine, sir; this house is mine, and I command you to leave it directly.

Marlow. Ha! ha! ha! A puddle in a storm. I shan't stir a step, I assure you. *(In a serious tone)* This your house, fellow! It's my house. This is my house. Mine, while I choose to stay. What right have you to bid me leave this house, sir? I never met with such impudence, curse me, never in my whole life before.

Hardcastle. Nor I, confound me if ever I did! To come to my house, to call for what he likes, to turn me out of

[1] **liberty and Fleet Street** Goldsmith, a Tory in politics, here satirizes the democratic furore then seething among the supporters of the political firebrand, John Wilkes, by putting their popular cry into the mouth of a drunken servant   [2] **banter** jest with

my own chair, to insult the family, to order his servants to get drunk, and then to tell me *This house is mine, sir!* By all that's impudent, it makes me laugh. Ha! ha! ha! Pray, sir, (*bantering*) as you take the house, what think you of taking the rest of the furniture? There's a pair of silver candlesticks, and there's a fire screen, and here's a pair of brazen-nosed bellows; perhaps you may take a fancy to them?

MARLOW. Bring me your bill, sir, bring me your bill, and let's make no more words about it.

HARDCASTLE. There are a set of prints, too. What think you of the *Rake's Progress*³ for your own apartment?

MARLOW. Bring me your bill, I say, and I'll leave you and your infernal house directly.

HARDCASTLE. Then there's a mahogany table that you may see your own face in.

MARLOW. My bill, I say.

HARDCASTLE. I had forgot the great chair, for your own particular slumbers, after a hearty meal.

MARLOW. Zounds! bring me my bill, I say, and let's hear no more on't.

HARDCASTLE. Young man, young man, from your father's letter to me, I was taught to expect a well-bred, modest man as a visitor here, but now I find him no better than a coxcomb and a bully; but he will be down here presently, shall hear more of it.   (*Exit*)

MARLOW. How's this! Sure I have not mistaken the house! Everything looks like an inn. The servants cry "coming." The attendance is awkward; the barmaid, too, to attend us. But she's here, and will inform me. Whither so fast, child? A word with you.

(*Enter* MISS HARDCASTLE)

MISS HARDCASTLE. Let it be short, then. I'm in a hurry. (*Aside*) I believe he begins to find out his mistake, but it's too soon quite to undeceive him.

MARLOW. Pray, child, answer me one question. What are you, and what may your business in this house be?

MISS HARDCASTLE. A relation of the family, sir.

MARLOW. What! a poor relation?

³ Rake's Progress engravings after Hogarth's famous series of paintings, showing the progressive ruin of a young profligate

MISS HARDCASTLE. Yes, sir, a poor relation, appointed to keep the keys, and to see that the guests want nothing in my power to give them.

MARLOW. That is, you act as the barmaid of this inn.

MISS HARDCASTLE. Inn! O law—what brought that in your head? One of the best families in the county keep an inn! Ha! ha! ha! Old Mr. Hardcastle's house an inn!

MARLOW. Mr. Hardcastle's house! Is this house Mr. Hardcastle's house, child?

MISS HARDCASTLE. Ay, sure. Whose else should it be?

MARLOW. So then all's out, and I have been damnably imposed on. O, confound my stupid head, I shall be laughed at over the whole town. I shall be stuck up in caricatura in all the print shops.[4] The Dullissimo-Macaroni.[5] To mistake this house of all others for an inn, and my father's old friend for an innkeeper! What a swaggering puppy must he take me for! What a silly puppy do I find myself! There, again, may I be hanged, my dear, but I mistook you for the barmaid.

MISS HARDCASTLE. Dear me! dear me! I'm sure there's nothing in my *behaviour* to put me upon a level with one of that stamp.

MARLOW. Nothing, my dear, nothing! But I was in for a list of blunders, and could not help making you a subscriber. My stupidity saw everything the wrong way. I mistook your assiduity for assurance, and your simplicity for allurement. But it's over—this house I no more show *my* face in.

MISS HARDCASTLE. I hope, sir, I have done nothing to disoblige you. I'm sure I should be sorry to affront any gentleman who has been so polite, and said so many civil things to me. I'm sure I should be sorry (*pretending to cry*) if he left the family upon my account. I'm sure I should be sorry people said anything amiss, since I have no fortune but my character.

MARLOW. (*Aside*) By Heaven, she weeps. This is the first mark of tenderness I ever had from a modest woman, and it touches me. (*To her*) Excuse me, my lovely girl, you are the only part of the family I leave with reluctance.

[4] **stuck up . . . print shops** the cartoonists of the period did a thriving business by selling caricature portraits of celebrities
[5] **Macaroni** fop or dandy

But to be plain with you, the difference of our birth, fortune, and education, make an honorable connection impossible; and I can never harbor a thought of seducing simplicity that trusted in my honor, or bringing ruin upon one whose only fault was being too lovely.[6]

MISS HARDCASTLE. (*Aside*) Generous man. I now begin to admire him. (*To him*) But I'm sure my family is as good as Miss Hardcastle's, and though I'm poor, that's no great misfortune to a contented mind; and, until this moment, I never thought that it was bad to want fortune.

MARLOW. And why now, my pretty simplicity?

MISS HARDCASTLE. Because it puts me at a distance from one, that if I had a thousand pound I would give it all to.

MARLOW. (*Aside*) This simplicity bewitches me so, that if I stay I'm undone. I must make one bold effort and leave her. (*To her*) Your partiality in my favor, my dear, touches me most sensibly; and were I to live for myself alone, I could easily fix my choice. But I owe too much to the opinion of the world, too much to the authority of a father, so that—I can scarcely speak it—it affects me. Farewell.   (*Exit*)

MISS HARDCASTLE. I never knew half his merit till now. He shall not go, if I have power or art to detain him. I'll still preserve the character in which I stooped to conquer,[7] but will undeceive my papa, who, perhaps, may laugh him out of his resolution.   (*Exit*)

(*Enter* TONY *and* MISS NEVILLE)

TONY. Ay, you may steal for yourselves the next time. I have done my duty. She has got the jewels again, that's a sure thing; but she believes it was all a mistake of the servants.

MISS NEVILLE. But, my dear cousin, sure you won't forsake us in this distress? If she in the least suspects that I am going off, I shall certainly be locked up, or sent to my aunt Pedigree's, which is ten times worse.

[6] **difference . . . too lovely** differences in social rank and fortune were then accepted as insurmountable barriers to marriage; Marlow's attitude here would have seemed proper to the audience, and his later proposal of marriage quixotically generous
[7] **stooped to conquer** "conquered" in the first version, and modified after Goldsmith had hit on the final title; see the Introduction, p. vi

TONY. To be sure, aunts of all kinds are damned bad things. But what can I do? I have got you a pair of horses that will fly like Whistle Jacket,[8] and I'm sure you can't say but I have courted you nicely before her face. Here she comes, we must court a bit or two more, for fear she should suspect us.

(They retire and seem to fondle)

(Enter MRS. HARDCASTLE)

MRS. HARDCASTLE. Well, I was greatly fluttered, to be sure. But my son tells me it was all a mistake of the servants. I shan't be easy, however, till they are fairly married, and then let her keep her own fortune. But what do I see! Fondling together, as I'm alive. I never saw Tony so sprightly before. Ah! have I caught you, my pretty doves! What, billing, exchanging stolen glances, and broken murmurs! Ah!

TONY. As for murmurs, mother, we grumble a little now and then, to be sure. But there's no love lost between us.

MRS. HARDCASTLE. A mere sprinkling, Tony, upon the flame, only to make it burn brighter.

MISS NEVILLE. Cousin Tony promises to give us more of his company at home. Indeed, he shan't leave us any more. It won't leave us, Cousin Tony, will it?

TONY. O! it's a pretty creature. No, I'd sooner leave my horse in a pound, than leave you when you smile upon one so. Your laugh makes you so becoming.

MISS NEVILLE. Agreeable cousin! Who can help admiring that natural humor, that pleasant, broad, red, thoughtless *(patting his cheek)*,—ah! it's a bold face.

MRS. HARDCASTLE. Pretty innocence.

TONY. I'm sure I always loved cousin Con's hazel eyes, and her pretty long fingers, that she twists this way and that over the haspicholls,[9] like a parcel of bobbins.[10]

MRS. HARDCASTLE. Ah, he would charm the bird from the tree. I was never so happy before. My boy takes after his father, poor Mr. Lumpkin, exactly. The jewels, my dear Con, shall be yours incontinently. You shall have

[8] **Whistle Jacket** a famous racehorse [9] **haspicholls** harpsichord, forerunner of the piano [10] **bobbins** shuttles used in lacemaking

them. Isn't he a sweet boy, my dear? You shall be married to-morrow, and we'll put off the rest of his education, like Dr. Drowsy's sermons, to a fitter opportunity.

(*Enter* DIGGORY)

DIGGORY. Where's the Squire? I have got a letter for your worship.

TONY. Give it to my mamma. She reads all my letters first.

DIGGORY. I had orders to deliver it into your own hands.

TONY. Who does it come from?

DIGGORY. Your worship mun ask that o' the letter itself.
(*Exit* DIGGORY)

TONY. I could wish to know, though. (*Turning the letter, and gazing on it*)

MISS NEVILLE. (*Aside*) Undone, undone. A letter to him from Hastings. I know the hand. If my aunt sees it, we are ruined forever. I'll keep her employed a little if I can. (*To* MRS. HARDCASTLE) But I have not told you, madam, of my cousin's smart answer just now to Mr. Marlow. We so laughed—you must know, madam—this way a little, for he must not hear us. (*They confer*)

TONY. (*Still gazing*) A damned cramp piece of penmanship, as ever I saw in my life. I can read your print-hand very well. But here there are such handles, and shanks, and dashes, that one can scarce tell the head from the tail. *To Anthony Lumpkin, Esquire.* It's very odd, I can read the outside of my letters, where my own name is, well enough. But when I come to open it, it's all—buzz. That's hard, very hard; for the inside of the letter is always the cream of the correspondence.

MRS. HARDCASTLE. Ha! ha! ha! Very well. Very well. And so my son was too hard for the philosopher.

MISS NEVILLE. Yes, madam; but you must hear the rest, madam. A little more this way, or he may hear us. You'll hear how he puzzled him again.

MRS. HARDCASTLE. He seems strangely puzzled now himself, methinks.

TONY. (*Still gazing*) A damned up-and-down hand, as if it was disguised in liquor. (*Reading*) *Dear Sir*,—Ay, that's that. Then there's an *M*, and a *T*, and an *S*, but whether the next be an *izzard* [11] or an *R*, confound me, I cannot tell!

MRS. HARDCASTLE. What's that, my dear; can I give you any assistance?

MISS NEVILLE. Pray, aunt, let me read it. Nobody reads a cramp hand better than I. (*Twitching the letter from her*) Do you know who it is from?

TONY. Can't tell, except from Dick Ginger the feeder.

MISS NEVILLE. Ay, so it is. (*Pretending to read*) DEAR SQUIRE, Hoping that you're in health, as I am at this present. The gentlemen of the Shake-bag club has cut the gentlemen of Goose-green quite out of feather. The odds— um—odd battle—um—long fighting—um—here, here, it's all about cocks, and fighting; it's of no consequence, here, put it up, put it up. (*Thrusting the crumpled letter upon him*)

TONY. But I tell you, miss, it's of all the consequence in the world. I would not lose the rest of it for a guinea. Here, mother, do make it out. Of no consequence! (*Giving* MRS. HARDCASTLE *the letter*)

MRS. HARDCASTLE. How's this? (*Reads*) Dear Squire, I'm now waiting for Miss Neville with a post chaise and pair, at the bottom of the garden, but I find my horses yet unable to perform the journey. I expect you'll assist us with a pair of fresh horses, as you promised. Dispatch is necessary, as the *hag* (ay, the hag) your mother, will otherwise suspect us. Yours, Hastings. Grant me patience. I shall run distracted! My rage chokes me!

MISS NEVILLE. I hope, madam, you'll suspend your resentment for a few moments, and not impute to me any impertinence, or sinister design that belongs to another.

MRS. HARDCASTLE. (*Curtsying very low*) Fine spoken, madam; you are most miraculously polite and engaging, and quite the very pink of courtesy and circumspection, madam. (*Changing her tone*) And you, you great ill-fashioned oaf, with scarce sense enough to keep your mouth shut,—were you too joined against me? But I'll defeat all your plots in a moment. As for you, madam, since you have got a pair of fresh horses ready, it would be cruel to disappoint them. So, if you please, instead of running away with your spark, prepare, this very moment, to run off with

[11] izzard an old name for the letter *z*

me. Your old aunt Pedigree will keep you secure, I'll warrant me. You too, sir, may mount your horse, and guard us upon the way. Here, Thomas, Roger, Diggory! I'll show you that I wish you better than you do yourselves.

(*Exit*)

MISS NEVILLE. So now I'm completely ruined.

TONY. Ay, that's a sure thing.

MISS NEVILLE. What better could be expected from being connected with such a stupid fool, and after all the nods and signs I made him!

TONY. By the laws, miss, it was your own cleverness, and not my stupidity, that did your business. You were so nice and so busy with your Shake-bags and Goose-greens that I thought you could never be making believe.

(*Enter* HASTINGS)

HASTINGS. So, sir, I find by my servant that you have shown my letter, and betrayed us. Was this well done, young gentleman?

TONY. Here's another. Ask miss there who betrayed you. Ecod, it was her doing, not mine.

(*Enter* MARLOW)

MARLOW. So I have been finely used here among you. Rendered contemptible, driven into ill manners, despised, insulted, laughed at.

TONY. Here's another. We shall have old Bedlam[12] broke loose presently.

MISS NEVILLE. And there, sir, is the gentleman to whom we all owe every obligation.

MARLOW. What can I say to him? A mere boy, an idiot, whose ignorance and age are a protection.

HASTINGS. A poor contemptible booby, that would but disgrace correction.

MISS NEVILLE. Yet with cunning and malice enough to make himself merry with all our embarrassments.

HASTINGS. An insensible cub.

MARLOW. Replete with tricks and mischief.

---

[12] **old Bedlam** very Bedlam; "Bedlam" was the popular corruption of the pronunciation of Bethlehem Hospital, the lunatic asylum

TONY. Baw! damme, but I'll fight you both, one after the other,—with baskets.[13]

MARLOW. As for him, he's below resentment. But your conduct, Mr. Hastings, requires an explanation. You knew of my mistakes, yet would not undeceive me.

HASTINGS. Tortured as I am with my own disappointments, is this a time for explanations? It is not friendly, Mr. Marlow.

MARLOW. But, sir—

MISS NEVILLE. Mr. Marlow, we never kept on your mistake, till it was too late to undeceive you. Be pacified.

(*Enter* SERVANT)

SERVANT. My mistress desires you'll get ready immediately, madam. The horses are putting to.[14] Your hat and things are in the next room. We are to go thirty miles before morning. (*Exit* SERVANT)

MISS NEVILLE. Well, well; I'll come presently.

MARLOW. (*To* HASTINGS) Was it well done, sir, to assist in rendering me ridiculous? To hang me out for the scorn of all my acquaintance? Depend upon it, sir, I shall expect an explanation.

HASTINGS. Was it well done, sir, if you're upon that subject, to deliver what I intrusted to yourself to the care of another, sir?

MISS NEVILLE. Mr. Hastings. Mr. Marlow. Why will you increase my distress by this groundless dispute? I implore, I entreat you—

(*Enter* SERVANT)

SERVANT. Your cloak, madam. My mistress is impatient.

MISS NEVILLE. I come. (*Exit* SERVANT)

Pray, be pacified. If I leave you thus, I shall die with apprehension.

(*Enter* SERVANT)

SERVANT. Your fan, muff, and gloves, madam. The horses are waiting. (*Exit* SERVANT)

MISS NEVILLE. O, Mr. Marlow! if you knew what a scene

---

[13] **baskets** foils with hilts protected by wicker guards [14] **putting to** being harnessed

of constraint and ill nature lies before me, I'm sure it would convert your resentment into pity.

MARLOW. I'm so distracted with a variety of passions, that I don't know what I do. Forgive me, madam. George, forgive me. You know my hasty temper, and should not exasperate it.

HASTINGS. The torture of my situation is my only excuse.

MISS NEVILLE. Well, my dear Hastings, if you have that esteem for me that I think, that I am sure you have, your constancy for three years will but increase the happiness of our future connection. If—

MRS. HARDCASTLE. (*Within*) Miss Neville! Constance, why, Constance, I say!

MISS NEVILLE. I'm coming. Well, constancy. Remember, constancy is the word. (*Exit*)

HASTINGS. My heart! how can I support this! To be so near happiness, and such happiness!

MARLOW. (*To* TONY) You see now, young gentleman, the effects of your folly. What might be amusement to you, is here disappointment, and even distress.

TONY. (*From a reverie*) Ecod, I have hit it. It's here. Your hands. Yours, and yours, my poor Sulky. My boots there, ho! Meet me two hours hence at the bottom of the garden; and if you don't find Tony Lumpkin a more good-natured fellow than you thought for, I'll give you leave to take my best horse, and Bet Bouncer into the bargain. Come along. My boots, ho! (*Exeunt*)

Act V

❦

SCENE I. *The House*

(*Enter* HASTINGS *and* SERVANT)

HASTINGS. You saw the old lady and Miss Neville drive off, you say?

SERVANT. Yes, your honor. They went off in a post

coach, and the young Squire went on horseback. They're thirty miles off by this time.

HASTINGS. Then all my hopes are over.

SERVANT. Yes, sir. Old Sir Charles is arrived. He and the old gentleman of the house have been laughing at Mr. Marlow's mistake this half hour. They are coming this way.

(Exit)

HASTINGS. Then I must not be seen. So now to my fruit-less appointment at the bottom of the garden. This is about the time. *(Exit)*

(Enter SIR CHARLES MARLOW and HARDCASTLE)

HARDCASTLE. Ha! ha! ha! The peremptory tone in which he sent forth his sublime commands!

SIR CHARLES. And the reserve with which I suppose he treated all your advances.

HARDCASTLE. And yet he might have seen something in me above a common innkeeper, too.

SIR CHARLES. Yes, Dick, but he mistook you for an un-common innkeeper, ha! ha! ha!

HARDCASTLE. Well, I'm in too good spirits to think of anything but joy. Yes, my dear friend, this union of our families will make our personal friendships hereditary; and though my daughter's fortune is but small—

SIR CHARLES. Why, Dick, will you talk of fortune to *me?* My son is possessed of more than a competence al-ready, and can want nothing but a good and virtuous girl to share his happiness and increase it. If they like each other, as you say they do—

HARDCASTLE. *If*, man! I tell you they *do* like each other. My daughter as good as told me so.

SIR CHARLES. But girls are apt to flatter themselves, you know.

HARDCASTLE. I saw him grasp her hand in the warmest manner myself; and here he comes to put you out of your *ifs*, I warrant him.

(Enter MARLOW)

MARLOW. I come, sir, once more, to ask pardon for my strange conduct. I can scarce reflect on my insolence with-out confusion.

HARDCASTLE. Tut, boy, a trifle. You take it too gravely.

An hour or two's laughing with my daughter will set all to rights again. She'll never like you the worse for it.

MARLOW. Sir, I shall be always proud of her approbation.

HARDCASTLE. Approbation is but a cold word, Mr. Marlow; if I am not deceived, you have something more than approbation thereabouts. You take[1] me.

MARLOW. Really, sir, I have not that happiness.

HARDCASTLE. Come, boy, I'm an old fellow, and know what's what, as well as you that are younger. I know what has passed between you; but mum.

MARLOW. Sure, sir, nothing has passed between us but the most profound respect on my side, and the most distant reserve on hers. You don't think, sir, that my impudence has been passed upon all the rest of the family?

HARDCASTLE. Impudence! No, I don't say that—not quite impudence—though girls like to be played with, and rumpled a little too sometimes. But she has told no tales, I assure you.

MARLOW. I never gave her the slightest cause.

HARDCASTLE. Well, well, I like modesty in its place well enough. But this is overacting, young gentleman. You *may* be open. Your father and I will like you the better for it.

MARLOW. May I die, sir, if I ever—

HARDCASTLE. I tell you she don't dislike you; and as I am sure you like her—

MARLOW. Dear sir,—I protest, sir—

HARDCASTLE. I see no reason why you should not be joined as fast as the parson can tie you.

MARLOW. But hear me, sir—

HARDCASTLE. Your father approves the match, I admire it, every moment's delay will be doing mischief, so—

MARLOW. But why won't you hear me? By all that's just and true, I never gave Miss Hardcastle the slightest mark of my attachment, or even the most distant hint to suspect me of affection. We had but one interview, and that was formal, modest, and uninteresting.

HARDCASTLE. (*Aside*) This fellow's formal, modest impudence is beyond bearing.

SIR CHARLES. And you never grasped her hand, or made any protestations?

[1] take understand

MARLOW. As heaven is my witness, I came down in obedience to your commands. I saw the lady without emotion, and parted without reluctance. I hope you'll exact no further proofs of my duty, nor prevent me from leaving a house in which I suffer so many mortifications.   (*Exit*)

SIR CHARLES. I'm astonished at the air of sincerity with which he parted.

HARDCASTLE. And I'm astonished at the deliberate intrepidity of his assurance.

SIR CHARLES. I dare pledge my life and honor upon his truth.

HARDCASTLE. Here comes my daughter, and I would stake my happiness upon her veracity.

(*Enter* MISS HARDCASTLE)

HARDCASTLE. Kate, come hither, child. Answer us sincerely, and without reserve; has Mr. Marlow made you any professions of love and affection?

MISS HARDCASTLE. The question is very abrupt, sir! But since you require unreserved sincerity, I think he has.

HARDCASTLE. (*To* SIR CHARLES) You see.

SIR CHARLES. And pray, madam, have you and my son had more than one interview?

MISS HARDCASTLE. Yes, sir, several.

HARDCASTLE. (*To* SIR CHARLES) You see.

SIR CHARLES. But did he profess any attachment?

MISS HARDCASTLE. A lasting one.

SIR CHARLES. Did he talk of love?

MISS HARDCASTLE. Much, sir.

SIR CHARLES. Amazing! And all this formally?

MISS HARDCASTLE. Formally.

HARDCASTLE. Now, my friend, I hope you are satisfied.

SIR CHARLES. And how did he behave, madam?

MISS HARDCASTLE. As most professed admirers do. Said some civil things of my face, talked much of his want of merit, and the greatness of mine; mentioned his heart, gave a short tragedy speech, and ended with pretended rapture.

SIR CHARLES. Now I'm perfectly convinced, indeed. I know his conversation among women to be modest and submissive. This forward, canting, ranting manner by no means describes him, and, I am confident, he never sat for the picture.

MISS HARDCASTLE. Then what, sir, if I should convince you to your face of my sincerity? If you and my papa, in about half an hour, will place yourselves behind that screen, you shall hear him declare his passion to me in person.

SIR CHARLES. Agreed. And if I find him what you describe, all my happiness in him must have an end.

(Exit)

MISS HARDCASTLE. And if you don't find him what I describe—I fear my happiness must never have a beginning.

SCENE II. *The Back of the Garden*

(*Enter* HASTINGS)

HASTINGS. What an idiot am I to wait here for a fellow, who probably takes a delight in mortifying me. He never intended to be punctual, and I'll wait no longer. What do I see? It is he, and perhaps with news of my Constance.

(*Enter* TONY, *booted and spattered*)

HASTINGS. My honest Squire! I now find you a man of your word. This looks like friendship.

TONY. Ay, I'm your friend, and the best friend you have in the world, if you knew but all. This riding by night, by the bye, is cursedly tiresome. It has shook me worse than the basket[2] of a stagecoach.

HASTINGS. But how? where did you leave your fellow travelers? Are they in safety? Are they housed?

TONY. Five and twenty miles in two hours and a half is no such bad driving. The poor beasts have smoked for it: rabbit me, but I'd rather ride forty miles after a fox than ten with such *varment*.

HASTINGS. Well, but where have you left the ladies? I die with impatience.

TONY. Left them? Why, where should I leave them but where I found them?

HASTINGS. This is a riddle.

TONY. Riddle me this then. What's that goes round the house, and round the house, and never touches the house?

HASTINGS. I'm still astray.

[2] **basket** see note on p. 1

Tony. Why, that's it, mon. I have led them astray. By jingo, there's not a pond or slough within five miles of the place but they can tell the taste of.

Hastings. Ha! ha! ha! I understand; you took them in a round, while they supposed themselves going forward. And so you have at last brought them home again.

Tony. You shall hear. I first took them down Feather-bed Lane, where we stuck fast in the mud. I then rattled them crack over the stones of Up-and-down Hill—I then introduced them to the gibbet on Heavy-tree Heath; and from that, with a circumbendibus,[3] I fairly lodged them in the horsepond at the bottom of the garden.

Hastings. But no accident, I hope.

Tony. No, no. Only mother is confoundedly frightened. She thinks herself forty miles off. She's sick of the journey, and the cattle can scarce crawl. So if your own horses be ready, you may whip off with Cousin, and I'll be bound that no soul here can budge a foot to follow you.

Hastings. My dear friend, how can I be grateful?

Tony. Ay, now it's dear friend, noble Squire. Just now, it was all idiot, cub, and run me through the guts. Damn *your* way of fighting, I say. After we take a knock in this part of the country, we kiss and be friends. But if you had run me through the guts, then I should be dead, and you might go kiss the hangman.

Hastings. The rebuke is just. But I must hasten to relieve Miss Neville; if you keep the old lady employed, I promise to take care of the young one.

Tony. Never fear me. Here she comes. Vanish!

(*Exit* Hastings)

She's got from the pond, and draggled up to the waist like a mermaid.

(*Enter* Mrs. Hardcastle)

Mrs. Hardcastle. Oh, Tony, I'm killed! Shook! Battered to death! I shall never survive it. That last jolt that laid us against the quickset hedge has done my business.

Tony. Alack, mamma, it was all your own fault. You would be for running away by night, without knowing one inch of the way.

Mrs. Hardcastle. I wish we were at home again. I

[3] circumbendibus roundabout route

never met so many accidents in so short a journey. Drenched in the mud, overturned in a ditch, stuck fast in a slough, jolted to a jelly, and at last to lose our way! Whereabouts do you think we are, Tony?

TONY. By my guess, we should be upon Crack-skull Common, about forty miles from home.

MRS. HARDCASTLE. O lud! O lud! The most notorious spot in all the country. We only want a robbery to make a complete night on't.

TONY. Don't be afraid, mamma, don't be afraid. Two of the five that kept here are hanged, and the other three may not find us. Don't be afraid. Is that a man that's galloping behind us? No, it's only a tree. Don't be afraid.

MRS. HARDCASTLE. The fright will certainly kill me.

TONY. Do you see anything like a black hat moving behind the thicket?

MRS. HARDCASTLE. O death!

TONY. No, it's only a cow. Don't be afraid, mamma, don't be afraid.

MRS. HARDCASTLE. As I'm alive, Tony, I see a man coming towards us. Ah, I'm sure on't! If he perceives us we are undone.

TONY. (*Aside*) Father-in-law,[4] by all that's unlucky, come to take one of his night walks. (*To her*) Ah, it's a highwayman, with pistols as long as my arm. A damned ill-looking fellow.

MRS. HARDCASTLE. Good heaven defend us! He approaches.

TONY. Do you hide yourself in that thicket, and leave me to manage him. If there be any danger, I'll cough and cry hem. When I cough, be sure to keep close. (MRS. HARD-CASTLE *hides behind a tree in the back scene*)

(*Enter* HARDCASTLE)

HARDCASTLE. I'm mistaken, or I heard voices of people in want of help. Oh, Tony, is that you? I did not expect you so soon back. Are your mother and her charge in safety?

TONY. Very safe, sir, at my aunt Pedigree's. Hem.

MRS. HARDCASTLE (*From behind*) Ah, death! I find there's danger.

* **Father-in-law** step-father

HARDCASTLE. Forty miles in three hours; sure, that's too much, my youngster.

TONY. Stout horses and willing minds make short journeys, as they say. Hem.

MRS. HARDCASTLE. (*From behind*) Sure he'll do the dear boy no harm.

HARDCASTLE. But I heard a voice here; I should be glad to know from whence it came.

TONY. It was I, sir, talking to myself, sir. I was saying that forty miles in four hours was very good going. Hem. As to be sure it was. Hem. I have got a sort of cold by being out in the air. We'll go in, if you please. Hem.

HARDCASTLE. But if you talked to yourself, you did not answer yourself. I am certain I heard two voices, and am resolved (*raising his voice*) to find the other out.

MRS. HARDCASTLE. (*From behind*) Oh! he's coming to find me out. Oh!

TONY. What need you go, sir, if I tell you? Hem. I'll lay down my life for the truth—hem—I'll tell you all, sir. (*Detaining him*)

HARDCASTLE. I tell you, I will not be detained. I insist on seeing. It's in vain to expect I'll believe you.

MRS. HARDCASTLE. (*Running forward from behind*) O lud! he'll murder my poor boy, my darling! Here, good gentleman, whet your rage upon me. Take my money, my life, but spare that young gentleman, spare my child, if you have any mercy.

HARDCASTLE. My wife, as I'm a Christian. From whence can she come, or what does she mean?

MRS. HARDCASTLE. (*Kneeling*) Take compassion on us, good Mr. Highwayman. Take our money, our watches, all we have, but spare our lives. We will never bring you to justice; indeed we won't, good Mr. Highwayman.

HARDCASTLE. I believe the woman's out of her senses. What, Dorothy, don't you know *me*?

MRS. HARDCASTLE. Mr. Hardcastle, as I'm alive! My fears blinded me. But who, my dear, could have expected to meet you here, in this frightful place, so far from home? What has brought you to follow us?

HARDCASTLE. Sure, Dorothy, you have not lost your wits? So far from home, when you are within forty yards of your own door. (*To him*) This is one of your old tricks, you graceless rogue you. (*To her*) Don't you know the gate, and the mulberry tree; and don't you remember the horsepond, my dear?

MRS. HARDCASTLE. Yes, I shall remember the horsepond as long as I live; I have caught my death in it. (*To* TONY) And is it to you, you graceless varlet, I owe all this? I'll teach you to abuse your mother, I will.

TONY. Ecod, mother, all the parish says you have spoiled me, and so you may take the fruits on't.

MRS. HARDCASTLE. I'll spoil you, I will.

(*Follows him off the stage. Exit*)

HARDCASTLE. There's morality, however, in his reply.

(*Exit*)

(*Enter* HASTINGS *and* MISS NEVILLE)

HASTINGS. My dear Constance, why will you deliberate thus? If we delay a moment, all is lost forever. Pluck up a little resolution, and we shall soon be out of the reach of her malignity.

MISS NEVILLE. I find it impossible. My spirits are so sunk with the agitations I have suffered, that I am unable to face any new danger. Two or three years' patience will at last crown us with happiness.

HASTINGS. Such a tedious delay is worse than inconstancy. Let us fly, my charmer. Let us date our happiness from this very moment. Perish fortune. Love and content will increase what we possess beyond a monarch's revenue. Let me prevail.

MISS NEVILLE. No, Mr. Hastings; no. Prudence once more comes to my relief, and I will obey its dictates. In the moment of passion, fortune may be despised, but it ever produces a lasting repentance. I'm resolved to apply to Mr. Hardcastle's compassion and justice for redress.

HASTINGS. But though he had the will he has not the power to relieve you.

MISS NEVILLE. But he has influence, and upon that I am resolved to rely.

HASTINGS. I have no hopes. But since you persist, I must reluctantly obey you. (*Exeunt*)

Scene III. *The House*

(*Enter* Sir Charles Marlow *and* Miss Hardcastle)

Sir Charles. What a situation am I in! If what you say appears, I shall then find a guilty son. If what he says be true, I shall then lose one that, of all others, I most wished for a daughter.

Miss Hardcastle. I am proud of your approbation, and to show I merit it, if you place yourselves as I directed, you shall hear his explicit declaration. But he comes.

Sir Charles. I'll to your father, and keep him to the appointment. (*Exit* Sir Charles)

(*Enter* Marlow)

Marlow. Though prepared for setting out, I come once more to take leave, nor did I, till this moment, know the pain I feel in the separation.

Miss Hardcastle. (*In her own natural manner*) I believe these sufferings cannot be very great, sir, which you can so easily remove. A day or two longer, perhaps, might lessen your uneasiness, by showing the little value of what you now think proper to regret.

Marlow. (*Aside*) This girl every moment improves upon me. (*To her*) It must not be, madam. I have already trifled too long with my heart. My very pride begins to submit to my passion. The disparity of education and fortune, the anger of a parent, and the contempt of my equals, begin to lose their weight; and nothing can restore me to myself but this painful effort of resolution.

Miss Hardcastle. Then go, sir. I'll urge nothing more to detain you. Though my family be as good as hers you came down to visit, and my education, I hope, not inferior, what are these advantages without equal affluence? I must remain contented with the slight approbation of imputed merit; I must have only the mockery of your addresses, while all your serious aims are fixed on fortune.

(*Enter* Hardcastle *and* Sir Charles Marlow,
from behind)

Sir Charles. Here, behind this screen.

HARDCASTLE. Ay, ay, make no noise. I'll engage my Kate covers him with confusion at last.

MARLOW. By heavens, madam, fortune was ever my smallest consideration. Your beauty at first caught my eye; for who could see that without emotion? But every moment that I converse with you, steals in some new grace, heightens the picture, and gives it stronger expression. What at first seemed rustic plainness, now appears refined simplicity. What seemed forward assurance, now strikes me as the result of courageous innocence and conscious virtue.

SIR CHARLES. What can it mean? He amazes me!

HARDCASTLE. I told you how it would be. Hush!

MARLOW. I am now determined to stay, madam, and I have too good an opinion of my father's discernment, when he sees you, to doubt his approbation.

MISS HARDCASTLE. No, Mr. Marlow, I will not, cannot detain you. Do you think I could suffer a connection in which there is the smallest room for repentance? Do you think I would take the mean advantage of a transient passion, to load you with confusion? Do you think I could ever relish that happiness which was acquired by lessening yours?

MARLOW. By all that's good, I can have no happiness but what's in your power to grant me! Nor shall I ever feel repentance but in not having seen your merits before. I will stay, even contrary to your wishes; and though you should persist to shun me, I will make my respectful assiduities atone for the levity of my past conduct.

MISS HARDCASTLE. Sir, I must entreat you'll desist. As our acquaintance began, so let it end, in indifference. I might have given an hour or two to levity; but seriously, Mr. Marlow, do you think I could ever submit to a connection where *I* must appear mercenary, and *you* imprudent? Do you think I could ever catch at the confident addresses of a secure admirer?

MARLOW. (*Kneeling*) Does this look like security? Does this look like confidence? No, madam, every moment that shows me your merit only serves to increase my diffidence and confusion. Here let me continue—

SIR CHARLES. I can hold it no longer. Charles, Charles,

how hast thou deceived me! Is this your indifference, your uninteresting conversation!

HARDCASTLE. Your cold contempt! your formal interview! What have you to say now?

MARLOW. That I'm all amazement! What can it mean?

HARDCASTLE. It means that you can say and unsay things at pleasure. That you can address a lady in private, and deny it in public; that you have one story for us, and another for my daughter.

MARLOW. Daughter!—this lady your daughter?

HARDCASTLE. Yes, sir, my only daughter—my Kate; whose else should she be?

MARLOW. Oh, the devil!

MISS HARDCASTLE. Yes, sir, that very identical tall, squinting lady you were pleased to take me for (*curtsying*); she that you addressed as the mild, modest, sentimental man of gravity, and the bold, forward, agreeable Rattle of the Ladies' Club. Ha! ha! ha!

MARLOW. Zounds, there's no bearing this; it's worse than death!

MISS HARDCASTLE. In which of your characters, sir, will you give us leave to address you? As the faltering gentleman with looks on the ground, that speaks just to be heard, and hates hypocrisy; or the loud, confident creature, that keeps it up with Mrs. Mantrap, and old Miss Biddy Buckskin, till three in the morning? Ha! ha! ha!

MARLOW. O, curse on my noisy head! I never attempted to be impudent yet, that I was not taken down. I must be gone.

HARDCASTLE. By the hand of my body, but you shall not. I see it was all a mistake, and I am rejoiced to find it. You shall not, sir, I tell you. I know she'll forgive you. Won't you forgive him, Kate? We'll all forgive you. Take courage, man.

(*They retire, she tormenting him, to the back scene*)

(*Enter* MRS. HARDCASTLE *and* TONY)

MRS. HARDCASTLE. So, so, they're gone off. Let them go, I care not.

HARDCASTLE. Who gone?

MRS. HARDCASTLE. My dutiful niece and her gentleman,

Mr. Hastings, from town. He who came down with our modest visitor here.

SIR CHARLES. Who, my honest George Hastings? As worthy a fellow as lives, and the girl could not have made a more prudent choice.

HARDCASTLE. Then, by the hand of my body, I'm proud of the connection.

MRS. HARDCASTLE. Well, if he has taken away the lady, he has not taken her fortune; that remains in this family to console us for her loss.

HARDCASTLE. Sure, Dorothy, you would not be so mercenary?

MRS. HARDCASTLE. Ay, that's my affair, not yours.

HARDCASTLE. But you know if your son, when of age, refuses to marry his cousin, her whole fortune is then at her own disposal.

MRS. HARDCASTLE. Ay, but he's not of age, and she has not thought proper to wait for his refusal.

(*Enter* HASTINGS *and* MISS NEVILLE)

MRS. HARDCASTLE. (*Aside*) What, returned so soon? I begin not to like it.

HASTINGS. (*To* HARDCASTLE) For my late attempt to fly off with your niece, let my present confusion be my punishment. We are now come back, to appeal from your justice to your humanity. By her father's consent I first paid her my addresses, and our passions were first founded in duty.

MISS NEVILLE. Since his death, I have been obliged to stoop to dissimulation to avoid oppression. In an hour of levity, I was ready even to give up my fortune to secure my choice. But I am now recovered from the delusion, and hope from your tenderness what is denied me from a nearer connection.

MRS. HARDCASTLE. Pshaw! pshaw, this is all but the whining end of a modern novel.

HARDCASTLE. Be it what it will, I'm glad they're come back to reclaim their due. Come hither, Tony, boy. Do you refuse this lady's hand whom I now offer you?

TONY. What signifies my refusing? You know I can't refuse her till I'm of age, father.

HARDCASTLE. While I thought concealing your age, boy,

was likely to conduce to your improvement, I concurred with your mother's desire to keep it secret. But since I find she turns it to a wrong use, I must now declare, you have been of age this three months.

Tony. Of age! Am I of age, father?

Hardcastle. Above three months.

Tony. Then you'll see the first use I'll make of my liberty. (*Taking* Miss Neville's *hand*) Witness all men by these presents, that I, Anthony Lumpkin, Esquire, of blank place, refuse you, Constantia Neville, spinster, of no place at all, for my true and lawful wife.[1] So Constance Neville may marry whom she pleases, and Tony Lumpkin is his own man again.

Sir Charles. O brave Squire!

Hastings. My worthy friend.

Mrs. Hardcastle. My undutiful offspring.

Marlow. Joy, my dear George, I give you joy sincerely. And could I prevail upon my little tyrant here to be less arbitrary, I should be the happiest man alive, if you would return me the favor.

Hastings. (*To* Miss Hardcastle) Come, madam, you are now driven to the very last scene of all your contrivances. I know you like him, I'm sure he loves you, and you must and shall have him.

Hardcastle. (*Joining their hands*) And I say so, too. And, Mr. Marlow, if she makes as good a wife as she has a daughter, I don't believe you'll ever repent your bargain. So now to supper. To-morrow we shall gather all the poor of the parish about us, and the Mistakes of the Night shall be crowned with a merry morning. So, boy, take her; and as you have been mistaken in the mistress, my wish is, that you may never be mistaken in the wife.

[1] **Witness . . . lawful wife** a burlesque of the customary form of legal oath

EPILOGUE

BY DR. GOLDSMITH

[SPOKEN BY MRS. BULKLEY IN THE CHARACTER OF
MISS HARDCASTLE]

Well, having stooped to conquer with success,
And gained a husband without aid from dress,
Still, as a barmaid, I could wish it too,
As I have conquered him to conquer you:
And let me say, for all your resolution,
That pretty barmaids have done execution.
Our life is all a play, composed to please;
"We have our exits and our entrances." [1]
The first act shows the simple country maid,
Harmless and young, of everything afraid;
Blushes when hired, and with unmeaning action,
"I hopes as how to give you satisfaction."
Her second act displays a livelier scene,—
Th' unblushing barmaid of a country inn,
Who whisks about the house, at market caters,
Talks loud, coquettes the guests, and scolds the waiters.
Next the scene shifts to town, and there she soars,
The chophouse toast of ogling connoisseurs.
On squires and cits[2] she there displays her arts,
And on the gridiron broils her lovers' hearts;
And as she smiles, her triumphs to complete,
Even common councilmen forget to eat.
The fourth act shows her wedded to the Squire,
And Madam now begins to hold it higher;
Pretends to taste, at Operas cries *caro*,[3]
And quits her *Nancy Dawson*[4] for *Che Faro:*[5]
Dotes upon dancing, and in all her pride,

[1] **We have . . . entrances** see *As You Like It*, II, vii, 139 ff.
[2] **cits** citizens   [3] **caro** beloved   [4] **Nancy Dawson** a popular ballad about a hornpipe dancer   [5] **Che Faro** "Che faro senza Euridice," the beginning of a famous aria in Gluck's opera *Orfeo*

Swims round the room, the Heinel [6] of Cheapside:[7]
Ogles and leers, with artificial skill,
Till, having lost in age the power to kill,
She sits all night at cards, and ogles at spadille.[8]
Such, through our lives, the eventful history—
The fifth and last act still remains for me:
The barmaid now for your protection prays,
Turns female barrister, and pleads for Bayes.[9]

EPILOGUE

TO BE SPOKEN IN THE CHARACTER OF TONY LUMPKIN

BY J. CRADOCK, ESQ.[10]

Well, now all's ended, and my comrades gone,
Pray what becomes of *mother's nonly son?*
A hopeful blade!—in town I'll fix my station,
And try to make a bluster in the nation.
As for my cousin Neville, I renounce her,
Off, in a crack, I'll carry big Bet Bouncer.

   Why should not I in the great world appear?
I soon shall have a thousand pounds a year;
No matter what a man may here inherit,
In London—gad, they've some regard to spirit.
I see the horses prancing up the streets,
And big Bet Bouncer bobs to all she meets;
Then hoiks to jigs and pastimes every night—
Not to the plays—they say it an't polite:
To Sadler's Wells,[11] perhaps, or operas go,

[6] **Heinel** Anna Frederica Heinel, a French dancer, had taken London by storm in the preceding season [7] **Cheapside** a plebeian market street in the heart of London [8] **spadille** the ace of spades, top trump in the game of ombre [9] **Bayes** a character ridiculing Dryden in Buckingham's *The Rehearsal* (1671), whose name became a comic synonym for an aspiring author, and in this context refers to Goldsmith himself [10] Joseph Cradock, a gentleman friend of Goldsmith's, who having read the play in manuscript proffered this unsolicited epilogue which Goldsmith printed, in an abridged form, out of politeness. The complete text, which refers to several features subsequently dropped from the play may be found in Cradock's *Literary and Miscellaneous Memoirs* (1826) I, 226. [11] **Sadler's**

And once by chance, to the roratorio.[12]
Thus here and there, forever up and down,
We'll set the fashions too, to half the town;
And then at auctions—money ne'er regard,
Buy pictures, like the great, ten pounds a yard;
Zounds, we shall make these London gentry say,
We know what's damned genteel, as well as they!

Wells a pleasure resort in the outskirts of London   [12] **roratorio** oratorio

BIBLIOGRAPHY

❧

TEXTS

The Chief Plays of Goldsmith and Sheridan, edited by O. J. Campbell. New York, 1926.

The Plays of Oliver Goldsmith, edited by C. E. Doble. Oxford, 1909.

The Plays of Oliver Goldsmith, edited by Austin Dobson. London, 1893, 1901.

The Works of Oliver Goldsmith, 5 vols., edited by J. W. M. Gibbs. London, 1884-86.

BIOGRAPHY AND CRITICISM

Baudin, Maurice, "Une Source de *She Stoops to Conquer,*" *Publications of the Modern Language Association,* Vol. XLV, 1930.

Bernbaum, Ernest, *The Drama of Sensibility.* Boston, 1915.

Black, William, *Goldsmith,* English Men of Letters Series. London, 1878.

Dobson, Austin, *Life of Oliver Goldsmith.* London, 1888.

Forster, John, *The Life and Times of Oliver Goldsmith,* 2 vols. London, 1848, 1854.

Gwynn, Stephen, *Oliver Goldsmith,* New York, 1935.

Hilles, Frederick W., *Portraits by Sir Joshua Reynolds,* New York, 1952, pp. 27-49.

Jeffares, A. Norman, *Oliver Goldsmith,* London, 1959.

Lucas, Frank L., "Goldsmith," in *The Search for Good Sense, Four Eighteenth-Century Characters,* London, 1958.

Prior, Sir James, *The Life of Oliver Goldsmith, M.B.,* 2 vols., London, 1837.

Schorer, Mark, "*She Stoops to Conquer:* a Parallel," *Modern Language Notes,* Vol. XLVIII, 1933.

Sells, A. L., *Les Sources Françaises de Goldsmith,* Paris, 1924.

Wardle, Ralph M., *Oliver Goldsmith,* Lawrence, Kansas, 1957.

The Collected Letters of Oliver Goldsmith, edited by K. C. Balderston, Cambridge, 1928. (See especially Introduction, section 5 and Appendix III.)